Giving Something Back

– CHRISTOPHER IRVEN –

An environmentally friendly book printed and bound in England by
www.printondemand-worldwide.com

FSC
Mixed Sources
Product group from well-managed forests, and other controlled sources
www.fsc.org Cert no. TT-COC-002641
© 1996 Forest Stewardship Council

PEFC
PEFC/16-33-415
PEFC Certified
This product is from sustainably managed forests and controlled sources
www.pefc.org

This book is made entirely of chain-of-custody materials

FastPrint
www.fast-print.net/store.php

Giving Something Back

Any similarity to any action person is purely coincidental

ISBN 978-184426-981-5

First published 2011 by
FASTPRINT PUBLISHING
Peterborough, England.

GIVING SOMETHING BACK

Christopher Irven

A solo unsupported cycle ride in the spring of 2010
to raise £23,000 for the Charity *Help for Heroes*,
equivalent to an indirect journey
from Land's End to John O' Groats and back,
a distance of 2,038 miles,
in one month

Total whole cycling days 31
Total whole rest and maintenance days 3

A pilgrimage is a paradox.
It is a journey towards an enduring purpose,
and the purpose is to be found in the journey

Acknowledgements

Without the support and encouragement of my family, this journey would not have been possible. First, I must thank Molly my wife who depends on me for care and support day and night. Not once did she utter a serious word of discouragement or concern about what arrangements were to be made for her care, knowing that if she had I would probably have ditched the idea. However, in the back of her mind, she knew she had given life to a quite remarkable brood on whom she could depend.

It follows that the next people to whom I am deeply grateful are my five daughters, because they took turns to look after their mother, cherishing her and then transferring her to the next on the list. The last daughter to give her a roof was Catherine who lives in the South of France. While there, in the last day or so of my journey Molly fell ill and had to be taken to hospital. This threw additional strain and anxiety onto a busy wife and mother of three young children. As soon as I reached home I took the first flight to join them there and she continued to care for us both until we were able to travel – at which point (Molly being unable to fly) her husband Richard drove us the 450 miles home to England.

Finally, there was the support of my two sons Paul and Andrew. Though he was in South Africa, Andrew alerted a school friend, James, who lived a few miles from the return route. He and his wife could not do enough for me when I spent a night with them. Then there was Niall, a friend of my elder son Paul, who met me on the road for a few miles and used his expertise to drum up public interest in the venture. Finally, there was the constant support of Paul and his wife Lucy to whom I phoned in daily accounts of my progress, which he then posted on my blog and sent out by email to around a hundred well-wishers. More often than not, these reports were sent late at night, but he dealt with them meticulously on the spot. He and Lucy also advised me on modifications to the route, and alerted *Help for Heroes* staff when I was due to arrive at Headley Court so they could meet me there.

No matter how self-sufficient a man might want to be, a journey of this kind requires a lot of back-up behind the scenes. Naturally, I only decided to go ahead when my splendid daughters offered to look after my wife; but I gave little thought to other matters such as publicity. All of that was picked up spontaneously by my wide-awake family and friends. It is only in retrospect that I realize how much I owe them.

Chris Irven

Contents

Introduction

In the summer of 2009, my wife Molly and I were watching a television programme about two soldiers who had been wounded in Afghanistan. Between them, they had lost an arm and three legs. They had been operated on in Selly Oak Hospital and then moved to Headley Court, the Services Rehabilitation Centre, where they had prosthetic limbs fitted and were taught to use them. In addition to the medical expertise, the support of their families was crucial. In the end they got their lives back. All they wanted to do was rejoin their units in some capacity or other, and stand to receive their medals. There was no hint of self-pity or resentment.

Molly and I discussed what we had seen. I said admiration from an armchair wasn't going to cut the mustard: I needed to do something, give something back. The next morning I decided on a solo unsupported cycle ride of 2,000 miles to raise sponsorship for Headley Court; and the charity *Help for Heroes* came to mind as the vehicle for spending the money. Later, one of my sons and his family came to stay and I asked his older children what they thought. They said I should go for it and they would rustle up support at school. Molly said I was getting old, I had never listened to her advice and was unlikely to start now; but if I came back in a body bag she would kill me. So I took that as a yes.

A week later, I bought a new bike. My old steel one had outgrown me, though the man in the cycle shop said that since buying it 14 years ago I had shrunk! I was outraged, so he measured me on a height machine. Clearly, it hadn't been calibrated properly because I measured 5 foot 9 inches instead of the 6 foot I had been all my life. But to avoid further humiliation, or an end to a beautiful friendship by calling in the weights and measures people, I bought a much lighter and stronger alloy machine. Then the detailed planning started. The family began working out online promotion and the plan gradually took shape.

Road trial of the bike

I decided to ride from home to Land's End, turn round and head for John O' Groats, and then back home. But halfway through the journey Paul, my son who was manning base and communications, persuaded me to return through London in order to visit Headley Court.

The route then resembled a distorted triangle of 2,038 miles. It didn't look much on the large map, all folded over on itself; but how far is 2,038 miles? Could I get a handle on it? Well, if I flew south from here for that distance I would be over the Timbuktu desert in the southern Sahara. Or if I were in Australia, it could take me from Perth to Sydney. But perhaps more dramatically, travelling that far south from here, Polaris the pole star would be 30^0 nearer the horizon: the stars would have shifted to a different part of the sky. We may not be able to move mountains but we can move stars if we try. And perhaps that was what motivated me.

I also knew that one didn't just move over a nice smooth surface of the globe: a lot of hills got in the way. On a previous journey of about the same distance, a conservative calculation was that the ups and downs amounted to at least 30 vertical miles, five or six times the height of Everest. This one would be about the same, and hills aren't only found in Scotland: the Cornish peninsular and the Northumbrian fells are exhausting too.

The three biggest factors, however, would turn out to be the relative wind, the road surface and the weight of the bike. Nothing could be done about the first two – the roads after the hard winter would be atrocious – and on a journey such as this with no back-up vehicle, the weight was always going to be a problem. Every eventuality had to be covered, including sleeping rough. The bike *was* heavy. This was my fourth such journey in 14 years and I knew it wasn't getting any easier. But I had deliberately set about telling enough people that I was going to do it to make chickening out unthinkable. I had burnt my boats. I was going to give something back.

The Plan

My Challenge on the Internet

"After 39 years' service in the Army, I have three times experienced the excellent treatment and rehabilitation offered to our wounded service men and women – in the Royal Army Medical Corps hospital at Woolwich, at Salisbury hospital, and by the staff at Headley Court which in those days was a rehabilitation centre for RAF personnel.

"I may be 75 years old now but I think it's never too late to try and give something back. Headley Court and Selly Oak Hospital desperately need extra funds for their work, so I intend raising money for *Help for Heroes* who are providing it.

"My original challenge, which began on 25 April, was to spend 35 days cycling from Land's End to John O' Groats and back, a distance of about 2,000 miles, alone and without back-up, carrying survival gear on the bike. This wasn't done to increase the money raised, because all your donations go to *Help for Heroes* anyway: it was to reduce the costs to myself which, even without the support vehicle, would be £2,700. The drawback was it greatly increased the weight of the bike, slowing me up. But the additional hardship was not unwelcome, for reasons that will become clear later.

“That was my original plan. However, having left John O’ Groats behind me on my way south, I was persuaded by my son Paul to extend my route, describing a huge triangle that took in Land’s End, John O’ Groats and through London to Headley Court in Surrey before returning home to Dorset. Headley Court now provides rehabilitation for all three of the Armed Services and I hoped to see the work they were doing for our injured servicemen from Iraq and Afghanistan. Headley Court is likely to be where much of the money I raise for *Help for Heroes* will be spent.

“Every penny you give – and a penny-a-mile is £20 – will be most gratefully received by *Help for Heroes* on behalf of our wounded service men and women. If you would like to help, please donate using one of the links below. On behalf of *Help for Heroes*, many thanks in advance for your support.”

Chris Irven

http://www.helpforheroes.org.uk/lejog-and-back.html

http://www.justgiving.com/Chris-Irven

Day 1: Monday, 25 April 2010

A Blessing And A Brainwave

12.00 hrs to 19.15 hrs
Odometer – 49 miles. Gillingham (Dorset) – Monkton (near Honiton) (49 miles)

After Mass, Father Martin asked me to bring in the bike to be blessed with me. He read a passage from the Book of Tobit, Chapter 5 verses 20-28: how Tobias took leave of his father and tearful mother with his father's blessing, under the care of Raphael the Archangel, to set out on his journey. Tobit had comforted his wife with the words, *'A good angel will go with him; he will have a good journey and come back to us well and happy.'* Father Martin then gave his blessing and we moved outside.

Of the family, Vicky, Fiona, Annabel and Andy with their two little girls had come to say goodbye. There too were my sister Janet, and family friends Rosemary and Adrienne, mingling with friends from the parish who crowded round to wish me good luck. Photographers from *The Blackmore Vale Magazine* and *The Western Gazette* took their photos and, escorted by

PCSO Pete and the owner of the cycle shop *Wheels* who had sold and set up my bike, we rode away, accompanied by cheers and (I was told later) even a few tears. We pedalled to the edge of the town where I said goodbye to my escort, and pedalled on towards the A303, my road to the west.

Farewell to Dorset

Before setting out I had had a brainwave that netted *Help for Heroes* £950 on the journey. I had made from white canvas a cross-sash from shoulder to waist on which '2000 MILES, HELP FOR HEROES' was written front and back. The effectiveness of this visible advertising of what I was about was already proving its worth, because when I reached the Sparkford Services I bought a burger for lunch and people young and old began giving me their loose change and asking what I was doing. On leaving the service station, I was approaching a lay-by in which a car had pulled up. The driver was out of the car and beckoned me to pull in, whereupon he gave me £5 having heard my story. He had been in the Fleet Air Arm and was enthusiastic about my challenge. From there on, many a time I was stopped, asked what I was doing and given money, and cars passing from time to time would signal support with a friendly 'honk' on the horn. All money donated was put into a purse reserved for the charity. Each evening I would tot up the day's donations and note them in my log; and at the end of the journey, I added up all the daily donations and sent *Help for Heroes* a cheque for the total. That way, I could spend the takings on food, keep and maintenance, thus avoiding the risk and weight of carrying an ever-growing amount of money in my front box.

During the afternoon, I started to get persistent and powerful cramps in my legs. I knew this would happen and had come prepared with quinine bisulphate pills. I also had to take these once or twice during the night: without them sleep would have been impossible. It was not until nearly the end of the journey that my body stopped retaliating with terrible cramps to the violence imposed on it. And this relief was probably largely due to the advice given me by James Baile (more of whom later) who showed me that bananas were nature's best cure.

There were two heavy but short showers that afternoon, a steady headwind, and some long gradients as I met the eastern edge of the Black Down Hills. Struggling up the longest of these climbs, I was overtaken and pulled over by my daughter Fiona. She had lent me a rather grand mobile phone so that I could take photos on the journey. I don't think she realized I had a digital camera, but even so that would not have offered the ability to transmit pictures each day. (My arrangement had been to phone my elder son Paul each evening with a report on the day's happenings. He would then type these into my computer – over which he had taken remote control – and transmit them to a pre-arranged distribution list of a hundred supporters.) My phone was steam technology or, in his words, Jurassic; but sufficient for the purpose I describe. What I couldn't do with mine or any other phone was keep it on while cycling, for two reasons: I would be unlikely to hear it over the noise of traffic; and even if I did I would not normally be able to answer it in time as I would need to stop safely, take my gloves off and so on. Towards the end of the journey I did try keeping it turned on in a breast pocket with the call set to vibrate rather than ring, but there was still the problem of stopping just mentioned. I admit this did limit its usefulness and missed calls were sometimes a problem.

Anyway, back to Fiona's wizard phone. She had given me a quick lesson just before setting off; but she had given me the wrong charger. As I was climbing the Black Down Hills she overtook me in her car and pulled me over. I was delighted and astonished to see her, and we swapped chargers. But when she found I had a dedicated camera and was not entirely at ease with the one she lent me, we decided to drop the plan of transmitting shots en route. She was, however, horrified at the hill I was climbing and the weight of the bike. I assured her this was nothing compared to some of the hills that lay ahead. Seeing I was wet and tired, she made me promise to find proper accommodation (as opposed to bivouac) that night – and subsequent nights until I had gained strength and the weather improved. We parted with a hug, and went our separate ways – I to the west, she east back to Gillingham. With a pang I realized that it would be my last contact with my family until I met Paul's family at Ampleforth on the return leg through Yorkshire.

So it was that, 3 miles short of Honiton, I found a good (and, I'm afraid, expensive) hotel in Monkton in Devon. I booked in, was shown to a palatial room, drank a full pot of tea with two more quinine pills, had a hot shower and came down for a double ham and eggs, $1^1/_2$ pints of beer and a carafe of water – still much dehydrated. It had been a tough introduction, though only half a day, and I was glad of a comfortable bed and good meal as the skies looked unpredictable and threatening. Cramps continued to assail me during the night until a fourth quinine pill finally allowed me to sleep.

Breakfast was simple, though I had to eat more than I wanted to stoke up for the day ahead. At that time the only other breakfasters were a middle-aged man and his wife. They were amazed at my undertaking. He was a keen cyclist but would not have dreamt of attempting it. Other guests came down and several times during the meal his wife left their table to ask me more questions. Finally, they gave me money for the charity. The hotel owner too gave me £20, equivalent to the cost of my supper the evening before.

As I left the hotel I met a tattooed and hairy biker coming in, encased in his black leathers. He could have been a Viking in a film set who had slipped away from the studio to buy some fags. We greeted each other cheerfully and he asked me where I was heading. When I explained, he too was astonished. I asked him to pray for me. His face lit up.

'You a Christian, then?'

'Yes.'

'I certainly shall. And I'll get my mates to do the same!'

Never judge a book by its cover.

Day 2: Monday, 26 April 2010

The Tramp And The Bishop

10.00 hrs to 19.15 hrs
Odometer – 112 miles. Monkton – Launceston (63 miles)

As far as terrain was concerned, this was a very hard day. More long hills were negotiated, as I skirted the North edge of Dartmoor. The bike went well, as did the legs with no more cramps. There was nowhere to bivouac on the A30 trunk road with continuous cuttings and embankments in this district, so once again it had to be a B&B – the last room in town. At a rough guess and based on my experience of my training circuit of 1,700 feet in Dorset, I estimate the ups (and downs) of today to have been around 15,000 feet. Consequently, I managed only 9 mph average – though compared to even tougher terrain I was to meet later, this was not bad. I stopped for a snack in a café and before long was joined by a Devon man and his wife. (Once again, it was the sash that had aroused curiosity.) We started talking about long journeys I had done, and why. I was given more money, and there was much hilarity, particularly when I told him about how I had once slept beside a bishop in Tiverton.

I shall now have to retell the story to you, dear Reader.

It was my first long-distance cycle ride 14 years earlier, effectively from Land's End to John O' Groats and back. On that journey, I slept rough much of the time as the weather was quite good and I was less tied to a schedule. Having passed through Land's End I was returning through Devon and had reached Tiverton on a Saturday evening as my night stop. Wanting to go to Mass in the morning, I found the Catholic church. The churchyard had a few large and rather pretentious tombs affording good shelter from the wind. I chose one quite near the pathway to the doors of the church, unrolled my sleeping/bivouac bag in the lee of a grave which also concealed me from the path, and noticed in the fading light that it was the last resting place of a bishop. An exalted tramp indeed: I was to sleep beside a bishop. I woke next morning as churchgoers were gathering on the path before the exodus of the congregation of the previous Mass. I crawled out, a dishevelled zombie, into view of the waiting faithful. In true English fashion they kept their questions to themselves – after all, we had not been introduced – and since there seemed little point in trying to explain why I had been sleeping beside a bishop, the least said the better. So I said 'Good morning,' and joined the queue for Mass. Catholics are a broad church, bishops and tramps on an equal footing, as indeed are all men in death.

As I went to the bike an old woman followed me out. What she said was difficult to understand but I gathered she had overheard our conversation. She kept repeating her admiration for the project, and pressed £4 into my hands.

I reached Launceston, a lovely hilly town with a pre-Norman castle and booked the last available room in the

Eagle House Hotel, a Georgian building of some splendour. The landlord was impressed by my story and gave me a £5 discount so I paid £35 for bed and breakfast. I then went into the town for a massive Indian curry to replenish reserves. Following advice, I am forcing myself to eat plenty – something that I have not been used to doing for years.

Cash collected today and yesterday £50.

Day 3: Tuesday 27 April 2010

Infinitesimal Yet Infinite

08.30 hrs to 19.30 hrs
Odometer – 181 miles. Launceston – Penzance (69 miles)

This was a very hard day from the point of view of endless and dangerous fast traffic; and what would, I was sure, prove to be the hilliest area of the whole journey – the Devon and Cornwall Peninsula. It seemed likely there would have been more hills (up as well as down!) on this 400-mile section than anywhere else on the journey. Yes, 400 or so miles, as the next day I should reach the south-west extremity and would have to repeat the whole journey thus far again, in the reverse direction, before heading for the Welsh Marches and the long run north.

My biggest worry cycling was wobbling about while climbing a hill on a narrow road, large lorries going past with inches to spare. Mindful of how the Archangel Gabriel (or was it Raphael?) had been sent to watch over the Holy Family on their flight into Egypt, every day I asked him to do the same for me. I also asked my readers to ask him too.

I had a lunch of fish and chips in a very good fish shop in Indian Queens (what a romantic Cornish name!) where more money was given me.

However, the day was not yet quite over. I was in Canonstown just short of Penzance, writing this log in the Lamb and Flag Inn where I was having my main meal of the day – a rump steak and a pint of Guinness. After that, I cycled on until I found a good hide in a reasonably level piece of ground, 4 miles before Penzance, and at 7:30pm stopped for the night. A ridge of high pressure seemed to be set fair. The temperature was 12C in a light south-westerly. The sea was "over there between the land and the sky," as Basil Fawlty had said to one of his more obnoxious guests, Mrs. Richards. And I was sheltered from view behind a brambly hedge, with the nearest house that could overlook me a good 400 yards away.

I selected the most level piece of ground, kicked away stones and stamped nettles flat. It was free of dung and rubbish. Nearby, a billboard had been set up inviting us to vote for change by electing the local UKIP candidate at the general election in a few days' time. I locked the bike to the legs supporting the billboard and off-loaded what I needed for the night. My rather thin sleeping bag was inside the Gore-Tex army bivouac bag that I had stolen from the quartermaster on returning from the Gulf War in 1991. It is the ideal alternative to a tent (with less bulk and weight) though a tent affords better protection from rain and wind. I put on a fleece and a wooly cap for extra warmth, and put the essentials into the bivy bag – water, anti-cramp quinine, head torch, pen and logbook, mobile phone, knife – and crawled inside. The night would not be unduly cold so I took off my cycling shoes before getting into the sleeping bag. They and other spare clothing were stuffed into a nylon bag to make a pillow. After writing my log, I phoned my elder son Paul who was very kindly acting as my editor to post my progress on the Internet. A quinine pill was swallowed, the draw strings of the bivy bag and sleeping bag adjusted to balance ventilation against heat loss, and I settled for the night. The whole operation of going to bed took 40 minutes.

Before going to sleep I squinted out of the ventilation hole and saw the stars begin to appear. This is always the best and most moving moment of sleeping rough. One feels infinitesimal, yet infinitely valued and loved by God. The experiences of the day come back to mind as the heart opens in prayer. I reflected that I seldom pray half as well when falling asleep in my own bed.

I was in sight of the south-west extremity of my journey.

Day 4: Wednesday 28 April 2010

A Psychological Start Point

08.00 hrs to 17:30 hrs
Odometer – 227 miles. Penzance – Land's End – Redruth (46 miles)

There was a little rain last night but not enough to wet the bag seriously. I slept well on the whole, even finding a shallow dip for my hip – an essential for a restful night – and at 6am woke and dozed. By 7am, reluctant to leave a warm bag, I crawled out, packed up (1 hour) and was away by 8am The hills were appalling. It was cold and dull, with a strong southerly wind. The gearshift on the chain wheel was playing up again, after only 190 miles. However, I caught sight of Land's End 15 miles away, resplendent in shafts of light piercing the overcast.

By 10am I arrived at Land's End, odometer 196 miles. Having reached this extremity of the island I felt as though my journey had now begun in earnest. This first 10% was more like a warm-up. The sun had at last begun to break through. I phoned home, had a sandwich and hot chocolate. Before long, I was hailed by some women from a Women's Institute holiday bus who had overtaken me on the road. Having discovered what I was doing, they unloaded their loose change and called over others in the party to do the same.

Land's End Gateway

I left Land's End at 12 noon and got to Penzance having located a cycle specialist. While he was tweaking the gears I spent an hour-and-a-half relaxing, writing and getting comfortable with a pint before mentally setting my sights northwards. I was under no illusions about the enormity of the task ahead. I reckoned 2,000 miles marked out on the surface of the globe would be 30^0 of latitude: heading south that far, the Pole Star would be 30^0 nearer the northern horizon and I would find myself in the southern Sahara. It was a dauntingly long way, I was getting a lot older, and there would be no room for ponceing about. I had to get my mind into gear and go for it.

With these resolutions in place, I went back to my cycle mechanic. He charged me nothing, and said he thought the chain would last the whole 2,000 miles. (On my last journey through France, the chain snapped at 1,600 miles, still 500 miles from home.) By 2pm I was on my way having decided to avoid Bodmin Moor. The A30 goes straight through the middle of it, but by taking the longer route around the north edge I could have an easier run. Anything to avoid the dangerous traffic and the endless long hills!

I reached Redruth and the lady in the post office gave me some phone numbers. One was a guest house at £30, which I found at 5:30pm after a long, hard day again. I had a Chinese meal for supper and washed my clothes before tumbling into bed. I didn't even remember turning out the light.

The cliffs at Land's End

Day 5: Thursday 29 April 2010

Fog And Forgiveness

08.00 hrs to 17.40 hrs
Odometer – 290 miles. Redruth – Launceston (63 miles)

As I recall the most physically demanding episodes in my life, two come quickly to mind – the Forbes Arête on the Aiguille du Chardonnay with my sons, a 19-hour day; and Mt Kenya in 3 days instead of 5 (very silly). Today was nothing like as bad, though it seemed so at the time: 63 miles on Bodmin Moor in continuous cold wind and rain over unrelenting hilly terrain in 10 hours. It shouldn't happen to a dog. But the difference was that today had not a single redeeming feature. The traffic was quite heavy, the mist impenetrable and every single garment was dripping wet. My supposedly waterproof Sprayway jacket was about as effective as a net curtain against the driving rain. My hands found that changing gear or applying brakes demanded real willpower. The cyclone's centre was to the south-east so I had a headwind all day.

At one point there was a multi-exit roundabout with no road signs. I had taken a road further back as an alternative to my planned route and now I was paying the price: I didn't know for sure which road I had been travelling. Taking a wrong turning now could add an hour onto this journey from hell. The mist was so thick that I had to walk down two or three exits to find which ones were straight and which on a curve. I then used map and compass to select the most likely exit from the roundabout – which looked worryingly newer than the date on my map. I cycled on for about a mile, peering into the murk for a sign. Suddenly there it was: I had got it right!

Even bad things come to an end and by 6pm I arrived at Launceston and headed for the Eagle House Hotel where I had stayed on the way down. They still had one vacant room! Luxuriating in a hot bath, I contemplated the day now quickly fading from my forgiving memory. Dry clothes were fished out of the waterproof sacks in my panniers and the wet ones taken to the kitchens for tumble-drying in the laundry. Food and wine completed the healing process and all the day's miseries were forgotten. (What a wonderfully forgiving person I am...) But I was thankful I didn't have to bivouac that night.

As I wrote up my log, I remembered other minor irritants of that day – such as when a bungee securing my luggage became unhooked and started winding itself around the rear axle, until the message percolated into my rain-soaked brain that the back wheel was incurring no ordinary rolling resistance. Mercifully, though, the spokes were undamaged. But the gears were misbehaving again when changing from first to second, so another visit to a bike mechanic was indicated.

I must get back to my brandy and ginger before the ice melts... Good night.

Day 6: Friday 30 April 2010

Junked Jacket, Junk Food

08.40 hrs to 20.00 hrs
Odometer – 359 miles. Launceston – Honiton (69 miles)

As Supertramp might have said, "it's raining again".

The clothes I had put in the tumble dryer the night before were damp but wearable so I put them on and went down to breakfast. I ate as much fruit as I could manage and then left the hotel. I pushed my bike through the keep of the Norman castle, the stronghold of the earls of that district, and joined the morning traffic until I joined the A30 heading east. The day was cold and rain had been forecast by the afternoon, but for the first time I had a 10 mph following wind. This made an enormous difference to my speed, and the Dartmoor hills were well manageable. The traffic noise was exhausting, particularly on concrete surfaces that extended many miles and produced a constant scream of white sound as the traffic flashed by. The gears and odometer were beginning to play up, so having made good time to Exeter I went to the Lloyd's Bank and topped up my phone with £100. While waiting in the queue, two women came up and gave me £6. The younger one got chatting, and it turned out she was a cyclist. She directed me to a specialist cycle shop not far away, so I took the bike there. They said it was due a good service of gears and brakes, quite normal at 350 miles. While there, I junked the Sprayway jacket I'd had for years and which had become useless. A beautiful Gore-Tex number replaced it, costing me a fortune, but I decided to put my health and comfort first for once.

The servicing was going to take about an hour, so I went in search of a meal. There seemed to be nothing between coffee shops on the one hand and very expensive restaurants on the other, so against all my principles I ducked into a 'Quick Food Outlet.' I wished I hadn't. Probably the quicker the food was let out the better, I pondered rather disgustingly. My bun's filling of compacted mince and plastic cheese tasted of vanilla and the bun imprisoning it had a cotton wool texture with no taste at all. The fries were like matchsticks and the best part of the meal was a bottle of water that took away the memory of each mouthful just long enough to make me dare try one more. The loud music also helped by numbing sensation and thought. How *can* the Americans come up with such a parody of good food? I returned to the comparative sanity of the street and back to the cycle shop, wandering around until my bike was ready. I then navigated my way out of the city.

With the wind behind me and on level roads, I pedalled on at good speed. As evening approached I cycled through a village near Honiton looking for a place to sleep out, but it was still raining and I couldn't find anywhere suitable. Besides, I also wanted a proper meal. So, faint at heart, I cycled back into the village through the rain and before long found a Victorian pub, The Orange Tree, doing B&B. I booked a room, locked my bike to a drainpipe in the alley and went straight to the bar for a pint. I was still wearing my *Help for*

Heroes sash and said good evening to four young men at the bar. Their conversation died away as I downed my pint before going up to my room to get out of my wet things and return to a small room at the foot of the stairs set aside for meals.

While waiting for mine, I started to write up my log. A little girl came and sat on the bottom step and stared at me. Her mother was the person who had booked me in. I was unable to write under such a penetrating gaze, so I put down my pen and asked her name. Loren said she was 10 and had had a good day at school. I asked what she had learnt. She said she was very worried about poor people in the world and was determined to do her best for them when she grew up. She asked me what I was doing and seemed pleased at my explanation. She then left to help her mother and I retuned to writing my log.

Two minutes later the four lads at the bar had crept up behind me and burst into boisterous song. One hand over my right shoulder gently removed the pen from my hand, another the log book from my left, and a third thrust a pint of bitter into my now empty right hand. We were away! I told them my story. One was in the Army, a Sapper, on leave. His brother hoped to join him before long. The other two were friends. More beer appeared, and my meal paid for, photos were taken. I felt exhilarated, and well boozed up. I explained I had to make an early start and they released me for bed. What a day it had been!

Tomorrow, Saturday, I aim to reach Downside.

Day 7: Saturday 1 May 2010

Monastic Hospitality

08.00 hrs to 16.00 hrs
Odometer – 413 miles. Honiton – Downside, Stratton-on-the-Fosse (54 miles)

I got up at 6am but breakfast wasn't to be until 8:30am so I left without. The air was still, the sky patchy with cumulus clouds and occasional sunny breaks, the air cold and visibility excellent. At one loo stop, I met an old codger of 70 who was recovering from cancer. His doctors had told him to take things gently so he had decided to do a solo motorcycle trip round France. We got on famously, laughing and joking about our experiences and our somewhat disrespectful attitude towards medical opinion, until a crowd of people gathered and emptied £56 into my bag. As we parted, he shouted after me, 'Just do it, Chris. Just do it!' That exhortation would ring in my ears on several occasions in the teeth of a gale or cycling up some interminable hill.

I made good progress until the A377 to Shepton Mallet took me off the A303. I was relieved to leave its screaming traffic behind and headed north into the Mendips. The Mendip hills are very tough – four high and steep ridges to climb, on one of which I had to get off and walk. Just outside Shepton Mallet the mother of all rain storms struck and I had to take shelter for an hour or so. Then, it was just a few more miles until Downside Abbey.

I arrived at Downside at 4pm and was met by André, the charming director of pastoral care, who showed me to my room in the monastery. I made my way to the abbey in time for Vespers, after which the headmaster, Dom Leo, welcomed me and took me to supper in the monks' refectory. Monastic meals are in silence, waited on by one of the monks. Tonight it was the turn of the previous abbot, a large apron over his habit. During the meal a monk reads, seated at a lectern. I was impressed to find that monks eat in haste, rather like the children of Israel at the Passover though without staves in their hands; but as I was very hungry I should have been able to keep up. Nevertheless, I became aware that the reader was glancing at me from time to time over the top of his glasses. Looking around, I was horrified to find I was the only one still eating. Hastily I put down my knife and fork and the reader closed his book. At once we all stood up, grace was said and we filed out to the calefactory where we enjoyed mugs of cocoa. The Abbot, Father Leo and some of the other monks whom I knew well, came and chatted with me most hospitably. We discussed the imminent general election, my cycling journey and other things, when Father Leo said I would be invited to say a few words about my journey, from the sanctuary after Mass in the morning. This provided a cue for me to thank them and say good night, and I went to my room to prepare my short spiel for the morrow.

I think tomorrow will be a very hard day so I would appreciate some prayers. Thanks.

Day 8: Sunday 2 May 2010

Mass At Downside, Bed In A Hedge

11.45 hrs to 16.00 hrs
Odometer – 413 miles. Downside Abbey – Pennsylvania (21 miles)

I was up at 6:15am, showered, sorted my gear and read over my short address to be given after Mass. I then made my way to the abbey church for the Benedictus morning prayer, after which Father Leo took me to breakfast. As always, this was in silence, but without the reader, and was self-service. I chose porridge, fruit and wholemeal bread and Father Leo brought me two boiled eggs with my initials on them "in case someone likes the look of them." After breakfast I phoned my own parish priest, Father Martin, to up-date him on progress and give my love to those at Mass. Next, I called Molly my wife who was due to be taken to the family of one of our daughters in Kent that day. (Without the kindness of my daughters who so readily looked after Molly, this journey would not have been possible.) Then I loaded my bike and went in to Mass in the abbey. The monastic community were there, of course, but also the whole school and many of the parents who were visiting their children for the weekend. The large church was just about full.

Mass was beautifully sung as ever by the monks and congregation. At the greeting the celebrant, former abbot Dom Richard Yeo, introduced the theme of the Mass and asked for prayers for me on my journey. He also said that the collection would be for *Help for Heroes.* After the communion, he asked people to sit down and invited me to come out and explain my purpose. I read my prepared address. The students must have been very attentive because, quite unexpectedly, they burst into spontaneous applause as I walked back to my seat. Dom Richard capitalised by saying that the applause signified their resolve to pray and contribute – and ask their parents to do the same!

After Mass I went to my bike with Fathers Leo, James, Nicholas and one or two other friends for a photo shot for the website, before saying good bye and heading north into the wind and gentle rain. It was already nearly noon so the distance covered today would not be great. After Radstock I took a wrong road and had to cut across a deep valley, partly on foot, to get back onto the Bath road. This set me back even more, and I abandoned hope of making a decent march that day. Instead, I had a good pub lunch outside Peasedown St. John and was on the road again by 2pm. A kind Yorkshireman from Doncaster pulled me over at one point and donated a fiver.

By 3pm I was climbing the long hill on the A46 out of Bath into the strong headwind. It was the weekend of the Badminton Horse Trials, I was warned at the pub, and every B&B for miles would be fully booked. Realizing I would have to camp, and making slow headway in the wind, I started casting around for woodland in which to bivouac. But I was getting onto the Cotswolds and the terrain was wide open. There would also be a lot of large estates ahead (the estate managers don't generally like vagabond cyclists kipping behind their high walls.) So when an hour later, 3 miles beyond Pennsylvania, I spied a hedge and dung heap, close to but hidden from the road, I took it. This would be my site for the night. Though hidden from view, it was unfortunately wide open to the north wind, which was cutting like a knife. It was going to be a hard night. I kicked and tramped a level-ish bed with a shallow 'hip-dip' and started to get organised. By 4:30 pm with most of my clothes on, I was in my 'bivy' bag with water, anti-cramp quinine, knife, torch, chocolate, mobile phone, log notebook and pen. As the ground was not very level, I put my near-empty front box inside the bivy bag near my head to stop me rolling while asleep. This is what I wrote in my log:

It's very cold – I warm my hands, undo a shoelace, warm my hands again and undo the other one. I'm now going to catch up on my journal and get some sleep, mindful of tough times ahead – the weatherman is talking about 17 mph headwinds and some rain for the next four days. I must keep praying that I hold my resolve. My sleeping bag is thin: a 4-season bag I deemed too heavy and bulky. Comfort has to compete against weight, and on this venture comfort will always come off second best.

I phoned Molly and members of the family including Paul 'my Editor son' with the day's SITREP, then fell asleep until woken at 9:30pm by a need to pee. What a palaver! Once back in the sleeping bag, I started to regenerate as quickly as possible the warmth I had lost. It was going to be a balance between suffocation on the one hand and hypothermia on the other. Inhaling oxygen from outside was necessary, but the exhaled breath had to be directed inside the sleeping back to minimize heat-loss. I realized I needed to breathe in through my nose and out through my mouth. And the nose had to be sticking out of the hooded sleeping bad. Simple. But you try keeping up that routine while asleep!

I woke again at midnight, stuck my head out into the wind and saw the stars: the sky was clear now. I prayed for the family, and for a dry night. After that I managed some fitful but fairly recuperative sleep until 5.30am. I had had worse nights.

Bivouac near Pennsylvania

Day 9: Bank Holiday Monday 3 May 2010

Somali Security In A Supermarket

07.30 hrs to 16.00 hrs
Odometer – 480 miles. Pennsylvania – Newent (46 miles)

Last night was cold – at least for England in the spring. I crawled out of my sleeping bag at 6am, teeth chattering, and put on nearly all the spare clothes that had been my pillow. I then packed the bike as quickly as I could; but even so, it took an hour-and-a-half before I was ready to start cycling. This will be common experience for anyone who has slept out in the cold but might surprise others. The cold slows every action down.

I hoped to find a lay-by with a caravan serving bacon butties and hot tea round about 9am but no such luck. Eventually I found a small fuel station where I bought a cocoa. The owner reminded me it was a bank holiday and Badminton horse trials would bring extra traffic.

All day I was hard pushed to average 8 mph into a strong headwind. I was already at least a day behind schedule and weather reports warned that the northerly wind would persist for four more days. However, it was dry and by 11am the sun came out to make things look cheerful. When I hurtled down hill into Dursley I found a supermarket, recently opened judging by the posters proclaiming the benefits it would bring to the town, and went in to see what I might buy for lunch. It was an enormous shop for so small a town and there were few customers. I locked my bike to a rail and noticed a security guard wandering aimlessly about the deserted aisles. He was dressed in a smart navy blue uniform and cap, a radio on his lapel to call for back-up if I cut up nasty. He was of African descent, probably Somali. I asked him if the shop had a café section with tables and chairs. Instead of answering my question, he looked at me challengingly and asked what I was doing there. I said that, strange to tell, I had come to shop, and repeated my question. He said he didn't know and hoped I would have a nice day. I suppose it could only happen in Britain. No doubt he was ticking an important box in the company's Ethnicity & Safety records. It was a harmless way of providing him with employment and might even have been saving benefit payments. I managed to find a pork pie and a bottle of orange juice and went to sit on the wall outside.

I then navigated my way round the south of Gloucester and took the road heading north-west into Herefordshire, intending to reach Newent by nightfall. As I cycled, I wondered how I might catch up on lost time. I decided to use B&B or hostel accommodation, as available, until I got back on schedule, since this would allow me to cycle later into the evening and save an hour's packing up in the morning. I was due to reach Shrewsbury by tomorrow night, Tuesday. That was about 67 miles; and I was hoping to reach Preston in

Lancashire by the end of Wednesday but it would be an even longer day of 87 miles. However, the going would be easier as the headwind was expected to drop from 17 to 12 mph. That may not sound much, but the wind force for good or bad is proportional to the square of the heading speed component. The square of the ratio of 12:17 is a half, so the wind resistance would drop by 50%. Not bad.

Incidentally, it was mathematical calculations such as this and other philosophical thoughts that would occupy my mind for hours on end, to help the miles slip by.

At last I rode into Newent and found a garret in The George, an attractive old inn. The day ended bright and breezy and I had a pleasant meal before going up to bed.

A tally revealed that I had received £156 in cash donations since the start, to add to the amount received through www.justgiving.com/Chris-Irven.

Day 10: Tuesday 4 May 2010

Unless You Become As Little Children

08.00 hrs to 19.15 hrs
Odometer – 559 miles. Newent – Hadnall (Shrewsbury)
(79 miles)

I left the George in Newent at about 8am and cycled 2 miles out of the town – on the wrong road. Spotting my deliberate mistake, I rode back into the town and picked up the route. The hills in Herefordshire are long but not too steep and the opposition of the wind – as predicted yesterday – had halved in strength to 12 mph. As a result, I had done 79 miles by the time I stopped in the village of Hadnall north of Shrewsbury. This was more like it.

The Hereford countryside, basking in sunshine, seemed to me the most beautifully English of any, a rural landscape at peace. There are villages where it seems the cattle, red as the soil, and the ewes are jumbled up among the crooked little cottages of brick and half-timber. There are authentic ancient pubs (one I rested at was 700 years old) where you are in danger of banging your head and the jukebox has found a niche where it can just fit out of people's way on the stone flags. The folk and livestock too seem to fit their timeless surroundings as if they had always been there through the centuries. Flocks of sheep in the dark green pastures suckle the new lambs with their tails wagging in ecstasy as they draw the warm milk. And so many different breeds! It's impossible not to burst into praise and thanks for such beauty. Even the names of the villages and hamlets betray their ancient origins: Little Marcle, Trumpet, Yarkhill, Hope under Dinmore. Some of the little black-and-white cottages look as though they have been thrown up by whatever materials were at hand, and by hands sure of their worth and the land that gave them birth.

I had been travelling roughly north-west. When I reached Leominster I joined the road running north through the Welsh Marches. The gradients were more manageable, compensating for the more direct component of the headwind. As I ran through Church Stretton I looked to my left where the low mountains of mid-Wales seemed to rise up unexpectedly just behind the town. These were the stronghold of the Welsh who had stubbornly resisted the English kings' lust for domination inherited from the Normans. To my right towered the Wrekin, as sudden as the Malvern Beacons. Then, after a few more miles, on my left again I caught sight of the Long Mynd (Mynydd Hir in Welsh.) On it lie the Stiperstones where 12 years earlier I had scattered the ashes of Iris my paternal aunt who had loved me – as she loved this ancient part of Shropshire. Along that windy ridge we had scattered them, where her heart was. She used to cycle and then walk there, the haunt of an ancient Celtic warlord who thundered by on his horse, seen by a few favoured and terrified travellers when the moon was high.

A little south of Shrewsbury I became aware of a longing for fresh fruit. As I rode through the village of Dorrington I spotted a Spar grocery, so I parked the bike, bought two large oranges and began to peel the first, standing outside the shop. The children were coming out of school. A young lad rode up, parked his bike beside mine and slowly walked around me as if inspecting a war memorial. I was wearing my sash, as always. Having completed his circuit he stopped in front of me.

" 'Scuse me. How many miles you riding?"

"Two thousand. It says it on the sash."

"That's a lot of miles. Where d'you come from?"

"Have you heard of Dorset?"

By this time half-a-dozen other schoolchildren had joined him. One of them piped up,

"It's by the sea in the south."

"Well," I said, "I've come from Dorset; been to the bottom left-hand tip of the country; turned round to head north where we are now. But I must keep going until I reach the sea as far as you can go. Then I turn right to the top right-hand corner of the country before heading south. I go through Yorkshire to talk to more schoolchildren there. Then I just keep going till I get home to Dorset."

Silence while it sank in. Then my first interrogator spoke again.

"You in the Army?"

"Yes I was."

"I'm going in the Army. And I'm going to be an uncle in 2 months. My sister's having a baby."

"That's great news!" I said. "How old are you?"

"Twelve years and two months."

"So you're going into the Army *and* you're going to be an uncle. That's terrific. What do you think the best thing is about soldiers?"

This time another lad piped up, quick as a flash.

"Looking out for your mates."

I was genuinely impressed. "You're dead right! Hit the nail on the head first time. If you remember that you'll be an excellent soldier."

Someone shouted out, "My brother's in the Army. He drives a jeep."

My friend pointed me out to the rest of them. "He's old, you know," he said in my defence. He must have spotted the beard.

A tall lad at the back had been listening intently over the heads of the rest of them. He reached into his pocket and gave me 23 pence. I thanked him solemnly.

"That's alright," he said airily, "it's for a good cause."

A little girl right at the front gave me a sticky five-penny coin. "Here you are, for the soldiers."

As suddenly as they had come, they were on their bikes and off, with cries of "Good luck!" and "See yah."

A dusky lad stayed behind. With great seriousness, he shook my hand.

"I'm going in the Army," he said. Then he too was gone.

I turned my attention back to my orange, but for some reason I now found it difficult to swallow.

By the late afternoon I started anticlockwise round the Shrewsbury bypass before regaining the A49 heading north. By the time I reached the village of Hadnall I had cycled 79 miles, and called it a day. I had a pint in the pub. More money was given, and there was some discussion about my project. They directed me to a B&B up the road, so I phone my son Paul with an account of a memorable day, clocked in at my B&B and returned to the pub for a meal. It was dark by the time I walked back to the B&B, and as soon as I got in I went straight to bed with a thankful heart.

Day 11: Wednesday 5 May 2010

Temple To Mammon In Wigan

08.15hrs to 21.00 hrs
Odometer – 644 miles. Hadnall (Shrewsbury) – Preston (85 miles)

The next day was the second longest of the journey, 85 miles. I was away by 8:10am in the rain which drizzled for 1½ hours. In fact it was dank and overcast all day. But the headwind was gentle. I reached Warrington, making very slow progress with dozens of lights, but the route-finding was going well. And then I got lost approaching Wigan. Some lads gave my position and, with my compass, I got back on the A49. My difficulties not over, I jammed the gears again on a hill. Losing the light, I had to cycle hard. Finally I got to Wigan. The problem then was to get out of it. In Wigan, the only signs are to Tesco's supermarket. In Wigan, it's almost impossible to avoid this great brooding temple with its serried ranks of worshiping cars. In the end, however, more by a process of elimination than anything else, I escaped Wigan and found Preston.

Things here were almost worse. I had no street map and relied on directions of locals. Four times I was given contradictory advice. This wasted several miles until I remembered the lesson I had learnt in Peasedown St. John: find a newsagent! They deliver papers; they know streets even better than taxi drivers do. Eventually I found my way to my cousin Caroline's house as dusk was falling, 9pm. Shamefully late. But you see, it was the pesky Lancastrian conurbation that did it for me.

She and her husband looked after me wonderfully, and rounded off a delicious supper of pork chops, leeks, carrots, cabbage and potatoes, followed by baked apple and then trifle and then, on hearing of my craving, extra fruit – I have a terrible craving for fruit. My son, his wife and youngest, Paul, Lucy and Hugh, had come all the way from Skipton to be with us at supper. This was very kind of them, but they must have got home very late. This brief contact with family and close relatives gave me a chance for some less superficial conversation. My son said I seemed small and frail but resolute.

Day 12: Thursday 6 May 2010

Shap

08.40 hrs to 19.15 hrs
Odometer – 706 miles. Preston – Shap (62 miles)

Today took me through Garstang, Kendal and the village of Shap 7 miles short of Penrith. To reach Shap from the south one climbs a long pass of about 8 miles. The pass summit is around 1,400 feet and is often blocked by snow in winter.

Since I last rode this way 14 years ago, the road has been engineered to make it less arduous. At that time on my previous steel bike, the torque applied to the pedals was such that the plane of the chain wheel became distorted and had to be replaced in Kendal. That bike, a Diamond Back was tough but less so than this lighter one. On that journey, apart from the chain wheel itself, I had to replace its bearing and the pedals, and later the front wheel bearing too. I also had one puncture despite having 'Slime' in the tyres. Today's bike has had none of these problems, touch wood.

After a Guinness in Kendal I started climbing, gently at first and then more steeply. The countryside unfolded below me and the headwind stiffened and chilled as I gained height. But it was enjoyable, a challenge eagerly anticipated. There were a few isolated farmsteads. The sky was bright, but clouds painted washes of dark shadow over the reds, greens and purples, and the brilliant pale yellow grasses of the fells. Sheep speckled the landscape in clusters, and the wind hissed and sang in the telephone wires. Tiny white or stone cottages could be seen here and there, and the occasional flash of bright tarns where water had collected in hollows. Birds fooled around on the wind like black scraps of paper, and the grey ribbon of road up which I'd flogged wound out of view far below. What a sight! I phoned some of the family to describe it. I contemplated sleeping out behind a dry-stone wall, but I had had nothing to eat and had expended much energy in the climb. So, having basked in the glory of that place, I mounted the bike and hurtled downhill at 30 mph for 4 miles through very desolate and less beautiful country, the wind rattling in my clothing, into the village of Shap. There I found a hotel with a roaring log fire and good food. A young couple, David and Ruth, enquired about my sash. They were fascinated by what I told them, asking many questions. Having put my bags in my room I went to the bar to order a meal. The barman told me David had told him to give me a meal on their tab! I ordered a lamb dish and paid for the wine myself, then went to thank David for his generosity. He asked for the H4H and JustGiving websites to give further 'support.' I then went back to the fire to eat my meal and phone the family. A superb end to a hard day.

Tomorrow I would be in Scotland.

A herd of deer in Cumberland

Day 13: Friday 7 May 2010

Lakeland From Across The Border

08.30 hrs to 18.40 hrs
Odometer – 783 miles. Shap – Dumfries (77miles)

The day dawned bright and very cold under the persistent northerly headwind. My left Achilles tendon is very sore, so in addition to the Ibuleve gel rubbed in generously, I swallowed a full-strength Cuprofen. This hefty anti-inflammatory cosh seemed to work and I made good progress. By the time I had rushed downhill from Shap I reached warmer air. The spring lambs were a constant delight, the hills gentle, the surfaces good and the sun began to shine. Earlier, I had come upon a herd of deer, some of them kissing their reflections in the river. The loveliness of distant fells gradually dropped behind as I powered northwards. It seemed the gods were smiling on me for once.

At 4:15pm and with 750 miles on the odometer I crossed the border. It was a sunny day and a delight to turn west on good roads and out of the incessant headwind. The result was that my cruising speed rose from 9 to 17 mph or even better. Before long, I reached Dumfries and found a B&B. Mrs. King welcomed me and said the charge would be £20 for bed and breakfast, or £18 if I went without breakfast. Feeling reckless, I opted for both. From my window in the bright evening, looking over the Solway Firth I could make out the Lakeland fells. I gaped in wonder at these lovely hills, which had taken me into their embrace at the age of 17, and remembered my happy days as a young man climbing them in summer and winter, sleeping on their tops and delighting in their green valleys cropped close by the incredibly hardy herdwick sheep. How I love these islands.

Day 14: Saturday 8 May 2010

The Soldiers' Mother And Mass In Kilmarnock

08.30 hrs to 18.00 hrs
Odometer – 837 miles. Dumfries – Kilmarnock (54 miles)

At breakfast, I and one other guest, Jo, were attended by Mrs. King. Mrs. King was a dear soul, only too pleased to take in the odd traveller on whom to unburden her thoughts. Jo too was most kind. She gave me a tenner for the cause. This was far too generous because she was clearly not on a great wage and had been sent away from where she lived to help at the local filling station. To my unaccustomed ear, she was also quite unintelligible unless augmented by lip-reading. It was one of those encounters where I found myself using smiles, nods, raised eyebrows and expressive sounds rather than words to respond to her remarks. I hope I did not seem too imbecilic.

I set off at 8:30am and was soon toiling up Nithsdale. As this ran northwest, I was once more heading into the wind. In the dale itself the trees sheltered me a bit, but once on the open moor it was so strong that even making 5 mph was difficult. I needed a rest, and at Thornhill found a farm shop with hot tea and a slice of shortbread and fudge. While recovering my breath, a woman in her mid-forties came up to my table.

"Are you doing this for the soldiers?"
"Yes."
"May I give you some money?"
"That would be very kind."

She pressed into my hands a small plastic cash bag used by banks, stuffed with some notes and many coins. Then she burst into tears. She apologised and explained she had three sons in Afghanistan. I stood up and gave her a hug. "Bless you and your sons, and may God bring them safe home," I said.

I sat down again and finished my fudge slice, much moved. Feeling she was uncomfortable and wanting to reassure her, I went over to the table where she and her sister were and asked if I might join them. At their invitation I explained what I was doing and why. We all ended up having a good laugh and then another woman came over and gave me a £10 note. Later, I found the plastic bag contained £29.19 . Incidents like this brought into focus in my mind the worth of what I was doing in a way I could never have foreseen.

I rode on. The going was level but the headwind unrelenting. The country was beautiful, green, wild, vast. The Lowland hills to my right and front, the Nith rattling or seeping by as the gradient took it, through huge green pastures speckled with sheep and cattle, between clumps of trees budding hopefully for the approach of a late spring.

At around noon I reached a rather dour little town, Kirkconnel. The street seemed to be lined by long terraces of low houses. One had a pub sign outside. Parking the bike, I went in and ordered a beer. Seeing the sash, the barmaid asked when I had started my journey. Before I could answer, a wag propping up the bar, sounding rather like Jazzer in the Archers, said "1941". Amid gales of derision, I looked tiredly at the barmaid and commented on the coarseness of the clientele – herself very much excluded, of course – to which she resignedly agreed. I then asked the bar in general if they could direct me to the quickest route back to England and civilization. More derision. The pub didn't serve food, so they gave me donations, one a fiver, and directed me (correctly!) to the nearest fish & chips shop.

At Auchinlech, I rang my daughter in Kent and her husband relayed the phone number of the Parish Priest in Kilmarnock, Fr Stephen Latham. He told me Mass was in 50 minutes at 6pm. Luckily, the ride of 12 miles was nearly all downhill so I got there just in time. After Mass, I asked him for advice on B&Bs but he insisted I stay at the presbytery and then gave me a meal, beer and coffee. We had a long conversation and found we had many common interests. I will always remember a large and beautiful print of the Crucifixion above his fireplace. It conveyed the lunacy and desolation of the event as none other I had ever seen.

Day 15: Sunday 9 May 2010

Across The Clyde

08.15 hrs to 18.15 hrs
Odometer – 910 miles. Kilmarnock – Carndow (Loch Fyne) (73 miles)

I left Father Stephen's presbytery at 8:15am and exactly 73 miles and 10 hours later, at the head of Loch Fyne, a hamlet called Cairndow, it started to rain. I could have gone further but was in urgent need of laundry, and found a welcome in a cottage beside the loch. So that was where I spent the night.

The going had been very comfortable on smooth tarmac, with only a slight headwind some of the time. I crossed the Firth of Clyde into the Highlands on the ferry from Gourock to Dunoon at 1:15pm. As I boarded the ferry, Chris de Burgh's sinister warning in his song *'Don't pay the ferryman!'* came to mind, and indeed the ferryman declined my offer of the fare. Furthermore, another passenger on board gave me another £10. At 2pm I stopped at an inn beside Loch Eck, had a light lunch and a beer. In the bar a group of men cyclists asked what I was up to and were a bit flabbergasted when I told them. Their day was to do the 19-mile circuit of Eck, Long and Holy Loch shores and the steep single tack through the forest connecting Eck and Long lochs, a very pleasant day's outing. When they asked how many miles I did per day, I said 70 was my average. Outside in the sun was a group of women on an 'activities' weekend of cycling and canoeing based at Beinn Mhór Lodge. News of my project got around and small groups detached themselves to talk about it and give me money. I collected £50 that day: my halt had been well chosen!

After lunch I reached Strachur on the banks of Loch Fyne and turned northeast towards its head. That led me to Cairndow ('Black Cairn') and the kindly Granny's guesthouse. Her husband kept a few cows and told me at one point that if they wanted cover for the night they would congregate at the end of their field and ask to be let into their barn. He loved them and said there was no sense in letting them get cold: they would only give him less milk. I thought that was rather nice. Granny had her granddaughter staying. She had travelled from New Zealand to look her up after 35 years. She helped her grandmother produce the most enormous tea reminiscent of the Yorkshire teas I used to have when a boy. I waited politely for someone to start but no-one did. It was then explained the entire meal was for me! I had to finish every crumb.

For the past fortnight there had been a constant pain coming from my left Achilles tendon. I was taking anti-inflamatories to little effect. I had been told it needed at least a day's rest but of course that was out of the question. However, I hoped to have that rest near Inverness with some friends while the bike had a thousand-mile service. But this had been a good day's mileage in 10 hours. Optimistically, I hoped it would mark a faster rate of progress in the future.

Sadly, it was not that simple.

Day 16: Monday 10 May 2010

Nor Looks Nor Mushrooms Kill

08.40 hrs to 18.00 hrs
Odometer – 962 miles. Carndow (Loch Fyne) – Rannoch Moor (52miles)

Glen Orchy

Loch Fyne's mirror-sharp reflections were just beginning to be ruffled by the breeze as I left Cairndow. I only cycled 52 miles that day owing to the return later of headwinds and some big hills. From Cairndow to Inveraray, then leaving Loch Fyne to climb the pass and down to Loch Awe. I paused for breath and coffee at a roadside caravan in Dalmally. The man suggested I follow the narrow track up Glen Orchy (it looks like a farm track on the map but isn't) rather than the longer and steeper way through Tyndrum. So

I did. It was a delight riding alongside the river to Bridge of Orchy.

I stopped at the hotel for some lunch at ten-to-three. At the bar, they said that lunch was on until 3pm so I went into the dining room and sat down to read the menu. A battle of wills ensued between two pretty waitresses and me. I had nowhere else to go and was desperately hungry so I couldn't afford to back down. There were just three tables of diners left, finishing their meals, and clearly the girls had decided that lunch had finished 10 minutes early. They clattered about on the parquet floor making themselves as busy as possible, avoiding my eye and willing me to leave. Eventually, the other patrons and one of the waitresses left, leaving the other waitress polishing the glasses furiously on the side table. She then collected them and took them to the bar in a Spanish rhythm of click-clacks. In my rubber-soled shoes, I padded quietly up and waited just behind her. It was 2 minutes past 3. She turned round and let out a little shriek of surprise. Had she still been carrying the glasses there would have been spectacular consequences. But she wasn't. My smile was seraphic as I ordered a salmon platter.

"The dining room's closed; it's ... 2 minutes past 3."

"Yes, and I came in at 10 to; and I'd like a salmon platter, please." So saying, I snapped the menu shut and handed it to her with a heart-melting smile and an icy gaze.

With a scowl and a coquettish toss of her pretty little curls she turned on her heel and click-clacked at speed to the kitchen. I returned to my table and continued writing my log. The salmon platter was held and held, in the hope I would crack and make a scene. Or perhaps she was looking for death cap mushrooms. I continued writing, blissfully uncaring of the emotional turmoil my beastly behaviour might be causing. Finally she broke cover, returning with the dish in a staccato of heel-clattering that would have put a Spanish flamenco dancer to shame. "Enjoy," she managed, through tight lips.

"I'm sure I shall. Thank you." I tried not to think of what she might have done to my salmon platter on its way to the table. But the meal was good, well worth the duel. I left the exact cost on the table and went out to my bike.

Whatever secret revenge she may have exacted upon me, I did not die a slow agonising death from some hideous fungus – and spittle I could just about handle. Besides, the food was vital for what was to come: a battle against wind and rain across Rannoch Moor to the Kingshouse Hotel. As I breasted Rannoch summit after 9 miles the wind hit hard in a sudden squall. It was icy, the rain and hail rattling on my hood and stinging my face. I looked down towards Glen Coe. The scene was like a Turner painting at the artist's most romantic – all swirling mist and strange light, rain and hail, with Buachaille Etive Mor dark and snow-streaked. I had deliberately chosen to take the longer route across the moor to soak up the atmosphere of this great empty wilderness, and it did not disappoint. Deep peat hags make its off-track crossing difficult and dangerous, a trekker's nightmare. In winter with unreliable ice and poor visibility, it would be a foolhardy venture.

A breather before Rannoch Moor

Luckily, the Kingshouse had a spare room. It was dilapidated and priced more on the hotel's reputation of remoteness than on its material comfort, I thought; but for me it was perfect. I had a shower, went to the bar and ordered a beer. "You're not paying for that; I am," said the barman. "And breakfast (£8!) is on the house." That set my gas at a peep.

I was now just a day behind schedule.

Rannoch Moor

Day 17: Tuesday 11 May 2010

Into The Great Glen

08.50 hrs to 17.10 hrs
Odometer – 1,023 miles. Rannoch Moor – Fort Augustus (61 miles)

Buchaille Etive Mor

I left the hotel and turned right towards Glen Coe. The road deceptively looked downhill but it wasn't: the well-known optical illusion of running downhill on a level road approaching high mountains was operating. The headwind was strong, but I knew the road truly steepened a mile or so on when I entered Glen Coe. Gravity must surely prevail, I thought. But it didn't. Brakes would normally have been necessary on this pass, but instead I had to keep pedalling in order to go downhill against the gale funnelled up the glen. Glen Coe is a special place for me. Memories came flooding back – ice-climbing on the Buchaille Etive Mor, the Great Shepherd of Etive, with my sons; sauntering on the fearsome Aonach Eagach with friends and not thinking too much about the drops either side; the strange Hidden Valley where cattle were concealed from enemies; and the treacherous massacre of a tribe. A Dark place, violent and beautiful.

Dropping hundreds of feet, the valley began to open out and the funnelling effect on the wind diminished. I reached sea level at Ballahulish and it warmed up slightly, but my hands remained numb. So I fished out my wristlets from my pannier and put them on, wasting quite a lot of time. I paused in the sunshine in Fort William and ate a pie before cycling on to Spean Bridge for a more substantial meal. Poised above Loch Lochy is the memorial to the Commandoes of World War II. This was their training ground. They stand tall and gaunt, gazing out at the wild snowy hills all around in which they honed their skills of endurance and survival.

The Commandoes' memorial, Spean Bridge

As I stood thoughtfully looking up at them, a young man and his girlfriend came up and gave me £10. I thanked them and was about to leave when two women and a man approached with donations.

"Are you from the West Country?"

"Yes I am, actually."

"Then you're Chris Irven. You've been featured on telly and in the Western Gazette. A bit of a celebrity."

I winced inwardly. "Goodness," I said.

"You see or hear about people doing such things but you never think you're going to meet them in the flesh. But here you are, at a War memorial the other end of the country! Very appropriate. Good luck!"

We chatted for a while and I discovered they lived in Somerset.

I had reached the 1,000-mile point. I mounted my bike and rushed down into the Great Glen. I reached Fort Augustus and found a most congenial couple running a B&B. It turned out they had known one or two monks in the Benedictine abbey there before it closed down. Their friends had now moved to another Benedictine abbey, Ampleforth, where I was due in 11 days' time.

The weather was still cold, now misty, and I longed for the arrival of a real spring.

Day 18: Wednesday 12 May 2010

The Loch, The Castle, And The Piper

09.00 hrs to 15.00 hrs
Odometer – 1,040 miles. Fort Augustus – Kilmorack (Beauly) (17 miles)

This was the day half-way through the journey set aside for servicing the bike, healing ailments, taking stock of progress and rescheduling if necessary. Rescheduling was indeed necessary. I had still not made up one of the days lost down south, and now my son Paul was urging me to go through London in order to take in Headley Court, the wounded soldiers' rehabilitation centre near Epsom. This would make the journey longer and more difficult but I could see it made sense; and after some thought agreed to do it. It involved a great deal of work to recalculate the route, make route cards and forecast the new arrival date. But the Shaw family who were looking after me in Beauly, just west of

Inverness, attended to my every need and not only made it all possible but a joy staying with them.

But I am jumping ahead. The couple owning my B&B for the night were Christine and Cameron. Christine was a most accomplished needlewoman who produced wonderful tapestries, some copied from pictures of ancient works of great beauty. Cameron was an academic who had followed various careers, picking up degrees along the way. It was 9am when our conversation was finally broken off – a very late start. However, I did not have far to travel that day so it did not matter.

Urquart Castle on Loch Ness

I had arranged to meet Donald Shaw at Dochgarroch and had reached Urquart Castle on the shore of Loch Ness just outside Drumnadrochit. The sun had come out and I paused to take a photo of the castle. While doing so, a voice behind me said quietly, "Hello, Chris." I turned round and there stood Donald in all his Highland finery, bonnet, cap badge, tartan, pipes and all: "We'll do some photos, I'll warm the pipes and then we'll collect a crowd". And so it was. After our own photos, the tunes began and then a crowd of tourists quickly gathered to listen and take photos of us! Donald stopped after a while and addressed them about my challenge.

The people chatted among themselves and an American woman asked me whether I had been in the Gulf War. "The first one," I replied. Then there were more tunes, ending with "Scotland the Brave" with me standing to attention beside the piper. More photos and a crop of donations followed.

Donald Shaw, Piper

After that, we drove to Inverness, bike on the back. (This was a major concession, a shortening of the journey by 28 miles. But Donald insisted and it would have been churlish to refuse his kindness.) We dropped the bike at the cycle shop and had lunch. Theresa and Josie were out taking their mother, Mary, who is 96, to the hospital for a body scan. After lunch, we picked up a perfect bike with a new chain and so on, bought flowers and wine for the girls and went back to join them for a lovely supper. Mary, however, had had a very tiring day and had gone to bed.

After supper my washing was done, an ice pack put on my worse ankle, and my log written up. I looked inside the study prepared for me where Donald had made up a convertible bed, and spotted a half-bottle of whisky beside my pannier. Such kindness, such thoughtfulness!

Day 19: Thursday 13 May 2010

Halfway Hospitality In The Highlands

Day spent tuning the bike and in make-and-mend. Odometer – 1,040 miles. Day spent at Kilmorack and Inverness (0 miles)

I understood a Blog had just been set up on the Internet to publish my daily progress. It is at chrisirven.wordpress.com and includes pictures.

The next day was a rest day, staying with Josie, Teresa and Donald at Tsitika, their lovely house outside the town of Beauly near Inverness. Teresa and Josie had decorated their gateway with balloons and flags in *Help for Heroes* colours. I spent much of the day eating and chatting with these good people. It served as a sort of recharging of batteries, both physical and psycho-social – just before I embarked on the loneliest two days of the whole journey. So I recorded in my blog my most profound thanks for all they did for me in those 36 hours.

Beauly and the surrounding countryside is an astonishingly beautiful part of Scotland, populated by some marvellous people. I wanted to go to church before continuing my challenge and Donald took me to St. Mary's RC Church, which offered a weekday Mass at a suitable time. Fr James Bell, the dean of the area, presided. I learnt from him afterwards that he was ex-infantry, poor chap. He was most friendly and we compared 'Army' notes. As a retired gunner, I had to field the inevitable brickbats from an infanteer. The motto of the Gunners is 'Ubique,' which means 'Everywhere'. Unsurprisingly, Fr. James translated it as 'All over the bloody place.' Much more surprisingly, his congregation collected £50 for *Help for Heroes*, a most generous act considering this was a weekday congregation.

I spent much of the day carefully working out the details of my new route from John O' Groats via Headley Court in Epsom, Surrey, back home to Gillingham in Dorset. So the overall route has expanded from LETJOG-and-back to a sort of huge triangle with Land's End, John O' Groats and Headley Court at its apexes. Maps had to be bought and marked, route cards prepared, and night stops estimated. A big task. I estimated passing through John O' Groats at noon on Sunday 16 May 2010.

That night the girls arranged a splendid farewell supper for me, and I went to my bed at 11pm, having finally completed my plans for the second half of the journey and phoned them through to Paul. Paul and Lucy had worked incredibly hard throughout to publicize the challenge, on top of their very intense 'day job' working for Mentor Initiative. I owe them an enormous debt of gratitude.

Teresa (right) and Josie's welcome – complete with Help for Heroes balloons!

Day 20: Friday 14 May 2010

Beside A Placid Sea

08.25 hrs to 17.50 hrs
Odometer – 1,112 miles. Kilmorack (Beauly) – Helmsdale (72 miles)

After breakfast I loaded the bike and walked up the steep drive with Donald, Teresa and Josie. Donald took one more photo. Then with a last farewell, I was off down the hillside and on my way. Two hours later I stopped for a coffee. One of the customers, an athletic middle-aged man, asked me what I was doing. He sat down and we had a long conversation about long-distance cycling. His preference is sea kayaking and I was amazed to hear that he can carry all he needs, including food and water, on a sea kayak. However, he is also buying a touring bike and so was interested in what I had to say.

I phoned Donald and thanked him and the girls for their unstinting hospitality and kindness in every way. I was sad that I had not been able to meet Mary, the girls' mother, who had been ill in bed. But Donald told me he had been sitting with her yesterday evening telling her about me and what I was up to, showing her photographs and so on. She was pleased and interested, and though in some pain, happy to be at home where she will be looked after well.

Today I cycled 72 miles in nine hours to Helmsdale. It was a respectable distance, and the most pleasant and easy day I'd had. It was not cold, the sun shone, the air was still, the gradients slight and the countryside beautiful and full of new life, spring lambs and budding green, a countryside at peace beside a placid sea. Every ewe seemed to have at least one new lamb. Furthermore, the traffic was light and my legs strong. My only pains were in my bum and, for the first couple of hours, my right shoulder and yoke. Even the road surface was good most of the way. The miles slid easily by, and before 6pm I rode into Helmsdale. My first choice of a B&B was full but I soon found an unpretentious and reasonably priced hotel, which gave me a good supper to round off the day.

I phoned Charlie Inness, at whose house I was to stay the following day. He said he would meet me on the Halladale road that morning at about 11 o'clock to take shots of me cycling in so desolate a landscape, and then lead me to his house.

Gold is panned in the Strath of Kildonan which runs to its mouth at Helmsdale

Day 21: Saturday 15 May 2010

The Northern Sea At Last

09.00 hrs to 15.15 hrs
Odometer – 1,156 miles. Helmsdale – Reay (Dounreay) (44 miles)

Today's start is as good as it gets. I rode out of Helmsdale on a good surface, the gold-bearing river running quietly to the sea through fields to my left. Sheep grazed in profusion in beautiful cropped pasture. White farms, protected from the wind by small clumps of trees, nestled between beige and brown hills, showing up clumps of cadmium yellow gorse. The sky was blue with a few cumulus clouds drifting north. And yes, the wind and sun were both on my back: for the first time that journey I had a following wind. Sad to tell, if it holds its direction after tomorrow it will once more become my enemy as I battle south. But it was ever thus.

I could hear curlew and (I think) lapwing calling, and occasionally a gaggle of geese would take flight complaining as I passed. I wasn't counting, but I reckon in 20 miles I met as many cars gingerly squeezing by in the passing places. As I climbed higher the view widened into the huge vistas of Caithness and Sutherland that I remembered from the last time here. Peat moors, with patches of blue water and gorse, stretched away to the lumpy brown hills. Some of these are quite high, though the lack of clear features such as farm buildings made judging distance – and therefore scale – very difficult. This was truly a land for bearing-and-distance navigation, with some resection possible here and there. Getting lost off-road in bad weather would be dangerous.

Aloneness – Heavy traffic in Sutherland

About half way I reached a station on the single track railway, with a hotel. I pulled in and asked for a cup of tea while I called Charlie. Before long, he arrived in an expensive Audi, brand-new. He handed me a lunch box and returned to the car to collect something. He came back a minute later and said he had a flat tyre. We set about jacking up the car and inflating the spare, and when the operation was well underway I went on ahead. He was going to catch me up and take action shots of me on the bike. With the brisk tailwind I hurtled along, but eventually he overtook me and took some good stills and video. He then drove ahead to sort things out at the house.

I cycled on; and towards the end of the road I topped a brow to behold the Orkneys squatting in a gentle blue sea. It was a psychologically powerful moment: I had nearly reached as far north is I could go. Turning east and with the wind behind me, I flew up to the village of Reay at 33 mph, the speed of a galloping horse. It was exhilarating and I felt like a god. I entered Reay and turned right up a bumpy track towards the house. Halfway along I noticed two enormous Clydesdales in the field. I propped the bike against a telegraph pole and went over to call them. They came plodding over, then stopped a couple of yards short of the low hedge. I reached over and called them again, hoping they would come closer. One of them stretched out his head and blew nervously at my outstretched hand but was still a couple of feet short; so, thinking him shy, I leant forward further. I was lifted off my feet. The strongest bolt of electricity I had ever experienced slammed through me like a tazer: my jacket had made contact with an electric fence partly concealed in the hedge. The horses flinched and then leant forward again, as if asking for an encore; and I could have sworn they were laughing at me, the rotters. They had lured me onto the fence. I may say I was wearing thick rubber soles and dry clothing, but it was no protection against 50 kV.

I cycled up to the farmhouse, a lovely home with spacious rooms tastefully furnished, and with out-buildings and some land. Apart from the two Clydesdales with the warped sense of humour that I had just encountered, they had other horses. I was introduced to their 12-week-old son Fergus. He is a delightful little chap. While getting me a cup of tea, Charlie wrote me a cheque for £60, a most generous gift.

Tamara had been away all day on an equestrian event of some kind, so Charlie and Fergus had had the house to themselves and had been doing lots of bonding and man-talk. Clearly, Charlie is besotted with his baby. Sadly, there have been two previous mishaps, so this little fellow is a great delight to them both.

Charlie cooked a very good supper and gave Fergus his bath, so that when Tamara arrived we sat down at once. We had a long discussion about the faith and Fergus's baptism, and their plans for the future. Tamara loves all things equestrian, and I told them about the electric fence. They roared with laughter and explained they had installed a fence with 'an industrial-sized kick', the highest voltage legally permitted, probably designed to keep out rhinos. Apparently the two Clydesdales, bored with their own company, had one day decided to go and talk to some sheep in the next field. A substantial wooden gate separating the fields had proved no impediment to their ambitions: they had simply walked through it, reducing it to match-wood. It had had to be replaced by a strong steel gate. That was when Charlie thought they had better make the whole field more secure.

I woke at midnight and went to the window. Still six weeks from the solstice, even without a moon the night was clear as on a heavily overcast day. I could see the distant islands, and in the field beneath my window the sheep were undecided about what to do: some seemed to be asleep, while others continued to graze. It reminded me how far north I had come.

Day 22: Sunday 16 May 2010

Followed By My Shadow

07.40 hrs to 16.40 hrs
Odometer – 1,221 miles. Reay (Dounreay) – Dunnet Head, John O' Groats and Wick (65 miles)

Dunnet Head light

I was on the road by 7:40am and cycled swiftly to Thurso, in still air and sunshine, not too cold. I passed through Thurso and just after Dunnet I turned north on a nine-mile diversion to Dunnet Head, the most northerly point on the mainland. It was a hard and hilly climb but I made it in good time. On the way, a couple overtook me slowly and then stopped some way ahead to take a video of me riding towards them. They gave me some money and learnt what I was doing. She asked my age, and was astounded that someone of that age should undertake such a journey. I stood on the headland, looked towards the Orkneys and Stroma. The sea, 300 feet below, was calm that day but we are told that in some of the raging storms that hurl themselves against the coast, pebbles are lifted high enough to smash the lantern of the lighthouse.

The 'official' photo at John O' Groats

After that I sped on as fast as I could to John O' Groats which I reached by noon as planned. I had the obligatory photo taken, then bought a hot chocolate which I drank outside in the sunshine. While I was being photographed, a small crowd gathered. Some of these came up to me later, giving me money and questions. One couple promised to donate online, being keen supporters of *Help for Heroes*.

Next, I cycled the 4-mile diversion to Duncansby Head, the most northeasterly point on the mainland. The stratified cliffs are impressive and provide nesting ledges for thousands of seabirds. One can see a line of stacks marching parallel to the coast a few hundred yards out into the sea. Like so many places on the coasts of these marvellous British Isles, these remote places are majestically beautiful.

On returning to the main road, I set off for Wick. The odometer was a little past the 1,200-mile mark so I had 800 or 900 to go. Having reached the apogee on my journey, I was filled with an enthusiasm and urgency to head south as quickly as I could. Adding to the feeling of having reached a turning-point, I became aware that the sun was now in my face.

For the first time I was being followed by my shadow.

I reached Wick in good time. The time was 4:40pm and – surprise, surprise – it had started to rain, the temperature dropping sharply as a cold front moved in. I was in the middle of a town, it had been quite a long day and promised to be another wet night. Growing soft in my old age, I looked forward to a hot shower and bed; so I decided not to bivy. The hotels were absurdly expensive, but after quite a search I found a B&B for £25. This was a bargain. It was run-down and scruffy, but so was I. We had a deal.

Duncansby Head, the most north-easterly point on the mainland, with the Orkneys on the horizon

Day 23: Monday 17 May 2010

A Labyrnthine Yorkshire Mind

08.00 hrs to 18.30 hrs
Odometer – 1,287 miles. Wick – Tain (66 miles)

This was a very hard day. Until I reached Loch Fleet at about 55 miles, the going was very hilly, especially the Berriedale Braes. These are always closed in snow, so steep are they. They are like a succession of ski jumps but far longer. Toiling out of Berridale, a passing lorry caused me to wobble, I lost momentum and had to stop. Once stopped on a steep hill, it is impossible to remount; so it was a long walk to the summit. And believe it or not, the headwind that had dogged me riding north had now swung south. I knew Zephyros was the god of the west wind but I didn't know the names of the north or south wind gods; so I asked Zephyros to pass on my displeasure to whom it might concern. I should add it had no noticeable effect. (It is meanderings of the mind such as these that help to pass the time for a cyclist stupid enough to embark on such activities.) However, I had in all seriousness prophesised this phenomenon to my friends in

Gillingham before I left. It followed the pattern of all but one of the long cycling journeys I had done. But even more infuriating was the speed of the change in wind direction. On the way to Land's End I had had a westerly; once I turned northwards the wind veered northerly, every day except one until I reached the north coast. I then had a respite of two days when it actually followed me. And now, as I headed south, the wind had swung southerly into opposition, right on cue. There was malevolence a-foot. The gods had it in for me, damn their eyes.

To add to my irritations, the odometer stopped working 6 miles out of Wick. I wasted half-an-hour fruitlessly trying to make it work. Until I could get it repaired or replaced I would have to rely on map miles for my log.

When I reached Dornoch Firth the gradients and wind relented – and it began to rain instead. By the time I got to the Royal Burgh of Tain, the rain had become heavy; so I found a B&B, clean and well-priced. To protect the innocent I shall call the owners Maggie and Keith, from Yorkshire. Maggie was friendly and very proud of her clean house which was packed with ornaments of every description – glass trinkets, iridescent pictures, soft (and hard) dolls, framed exhortations to be happy and kind, elaborately embroidered draught excluders, a glockenspiel in one corner, little creatures that had come in from the cold and stayed ever since, and an enormous bear that had got to my bed before I did, a sort of Goldilocks situation in reverse. Dear Maggie said I looked thin and when had I last eaten. I said at breakfast, and she told me to skedaddle to the town for a meal before everything closed. I did, and had a superb meal of soup, sea bass, cheesecake and 2 glasses of Merlot, seated in a rather grand hotel restaurant with a view of the town's clock tower.

On returning to the house I parked my bike under the roof of a spacious open garage with a corrugated roof. There was a car there, so I leant the bike against the back wall, well clear. As I came out from the overhead cover I was confronted by Keith. I reckoned he was in his seventies.

His first words were, "Where's tha' put bike?"

I felt as if I had stolen it. So I owned up.

"We'll not have bike near t' car overnight," he said, and went to move it into the back garden.

I wondered whether he was afraid the car and bike would get up to some hanky-panky once our backs were turned, and be found in the morning light looking sheepish, having produced some ghastly cross-bred two-stroke motor scooter. I was still pondering the labyrinthine workings of the Yorkshire mind when Maggie interrupted and insisted on walking me round every room in her house, to admire the view from each window.

In the morning I was up before Maggie or Keith and had noticed a bowl of fruit in the kitchen. Having loaded the bike, I went back to the kitchen where the two of them were busy. I cheerfully wished them good morning. Keith looked sharply at me, his mouth slightly open and a look of astonishment and disapproval on his face. Clearly, I had overstepped the mark: I had spoken before being spoken to. Looking him firmly in the eye, I repeated my greeting more loudly. This elicited a grudging acknowledgement from Keith.

"Good," I said airily, "I wondered if I might have some fruit instead of cereal." So saying and without waiting for a reply, I helped myself to 2 pears and took them back to the breakfast room. Keith was rather taken aback by this guest who seemed to know neither his place nor when to be intimidated. He reappeared in the breakfast room and in more subdued tones took the rest of my breakfast order. I was charm itself, cheerfully grateful for everything he brought me. When I finally left he wished me safe journey and advised me to take special care on the A9. I even managed to make him laugh with some wisecrack before we said goodbye, and he seemed genuinely pleased to have met someone at last who gave as good as he got.

Day 24: Tuesday 18 May 2010

The Pilgrimage Purpose Revealed

08.00 hrs to 16.15 hrs
Odometer – 1,354 miles. Tain – Aviemore (67 miles)

The sun was warming up and there was no wind. After 30 minutes I took off my waterproof and jersey. I made rapid progress for 10 miles and then began the climb up and over the Black Isle before swooping down over the bridge at Inverness. Almost at once the long gradients started. I found a suitable gear and toiled on, trying not to notice the pain, which began around my Achilles tendon. My speed settled at 6½ mph as the hills stretched endlessly mile after mile. At the top of every uphill stretch of one to 3 miles, the loathsome down-gradient would send me hurtling into a valley. I deeply resented these down gradients. They afforded some short-term relief, while robbing me of much of my hard-won altitude. In my mind, I compared them to the behaviour of our spendthrift Labour Government frittering away our hard-earned taxes to curry favour from a wavering electorate. I decided that I detested and despised both the hills and the Government – though probably the hills twice as much.

At 3:10pm I finally breasted Slochd Summit, just 80 feet lower then Shap Pass. Then began the descent towards Aviemore, this time with no more taxation from intervening hills. I saw ahead of me the bulk of the Cairngorm mountains, well covered in snow, as I knew they would be. On all of my previous "pilgrimages" I have remarked that at some point well into the journey the true motive for setting out comes clear to the mind. This happened today, only this time I had foreseen the reason from the start, albeit vaguely. As I approached Slochd Summit and the massive white bulk of the Cairngorm group became framed between the pine trees lining the road, I was acutely aware of a constant level of suffering, day after day, taken on willingly as part of the deal. Then I asked myself why I had undertaken this challenge. I looked for a succinct sentence or phrase, and at once it came to me: "for the soldiers, loving compassion." It sounded rather high-flown, but actually it wasn't; it exactly summed up my reasons. I admired them, honoured them. In short, I loved them. I wanted in some small way to share their pain borne for me and millions of others. And I had; I was; I would. Those five words that came to me were the key to my pilgrimage. A Christian calls loving compassion 'carrying the Cross.' High-flown it may or may not sound, but down-to-earth it certainly is – messy, sweaty, sometimes even bloody.

Even as I reached this conclusion, I became aware of a new source of pain vying for my attention. The soles of my feet had begun to throb and burn. They had to be turned off. "Hello, soles of my feet," I shouted to the passing traffic. "Your complaint has been duly noted. Now piss off." I realized, not for the first time, that I was talking to myself – or in this case, to the soles of my feet. Clearly, the hills had taken their toll: I was unhinged.

On reaching Aviemore, I couldn't find any bed for under £70 so the Information Bureau directed me to the Youth

Hostel for a bed in a dormitory, which was fine. How was I feeling that day? In low spirits first thing in the morning, very sorry for myself; picked up a bit in the afternoon. At the YHA, I attempted to send an email in a time-limited session on the hostel computer and my spirits took another knock. Without warning and with no opportunity to save or print the work done, the computer suddenly cut out. This effectively wasted the £3 and all the time I had spent writing my log to email to Paul. A meaner-spirited set-up I could scarcely imagine. Tomorrow, I would stop in Pitlochry, short of Perth, as I heard there was a cycle shop there where I might buy a new odometer.

HERE IS A CLIPPING FROM THE SCOTTISH PRESS OF MONDAY 17TH MAY 2010

POSTED ON THE BLOG ON 23RD MAY 2010

A HERO FOR HEROES

Retired Dorset Army major cycles length of Britain for wounded soldiers

A pensioner who served in the army for 39 years is more than half way through an epic 2,000 mile cycle from Land's End to John O' Groats and back.

Chris Irven, 75, a retired army major, who has also struggled against chronic leukemia, has suffered a near-fatal car accident and survived a minor stroke, set out on the challenge last month from his home town of Gillingham, North Dorset, in a bid to raise money for *Help for Heroes*.

The father of seven cycled from Gillingham to Land's End, then back up through Bath, Gloucester and the west side of the Mainland, up to the Lake District, then on to Scotland, arriving in John O' Groats on Sunday.

He will now head South through Scotland, the Northeast of England and down through London before arriving back home in Gillingham on or around May 29.

As part of the journey Chris plans to stop off at Headley Court, the military rehabilitation centre in Epsom, Surrey, where he was treated while he served in the army.

Chris said: "Last year my wife and I watched the TV documentary Wounded.

"We were enormously impressed by the resolute courage not only of the two soldiers but also of their families and friends, and the skill and dedication of the doctors and rehabilitation specialists who helped them get their lives back in a very real sense.

"The men themselves had no room for resentment or self-pity; just a burning resolve to get back on whatever feet were provided for them and stand to receive their medals with their comrades. And then if possible to rejoin their units in some capacity or other.

"Theirs is the kind of courage that inspires a nation. I resolved there and then to get out of my armchair and do something.

"So I decided to do a long-distance cycle ride, but with a difference. I would imitate in some small way the self-reliance and determination of these young men and women of whom we are so justly proud."

He added: "I don't want to 'come the Old Soldier', but I did 39 years' service in the Army and have three times experienced the excellent treatment and rehabilitation offered to our wounded service men and women – in the Royal Army Medical Corps hospital at Woolwich, at Salisbury hospital, and by the staff at Headley Court which in those days was a rehabilitation centre for RAF personnel.

"I may be 75 years old now but I think it's never too late to try and give something back. Headley Court and Selly Oak Hospital desperately need extra funds for their work, so I aim to raise money for *Help for Heroes* which is providing much of it."

Chris has been cycling solo throughout the journey without a support vehicle or back-up team, and has often slept rough in an old army bivouac bag or with the permission of the local priest in church presbyteries en route.

Writing in his blog on Monday after reaching Tain north of Inverness, Chris said: "It's been a very hard, exhausting, day. There were huge gradients until mile 55 when it flattened out somewhat.

"There's been a wretched headwind all day and it's been sapping my strength and my morale, but I've made it anyway. It's really lowered my spirits – I've been feeling very low, but I've recovered now, after a good meal and a whisky.

"Seldom have I felt so pleased to find a bed for the night and a good meal. It's been an exhausting day, in every sense, but I'm still on schedule and I really must avoid gradients in future."

So far in his journey, Chris has raised more than £6,000 for *Help for Heroes*. To sponsor him go to

www.justgiving.com/Chris-Irven. To keep up to date with Chris's progress read his blog at

http://chrisirven.wordpress.com.

Help for Heroes provides practical direct support to those servicemen and women wounded in the line of duty in the current conflicts in Iraq and Afghanistan. For more information visit

www.helpforheroes.org.uk.

At this point in the account published in the Internet blog, my son Paul included the following text and pictures:

SOME PICTURES OF A JURASSIC MOUNTAINEER

Ed: I have taken the liberty of attaching a collage from the "middle era" of Chris' climbing. This was in Chamonix Mont Blanc with second son Andrew and his friend, Nick, c. 1990. I'll upload the original photos to the blog later. Chris doesn't yet know about this – I hope I won't regret it.

Climbing in 1990 – pics from the archive

We found these pictures from the archive of Chris climbing in another era, 20 years ago. Even then, his gear was Jurassic. Commentary from his son Andrew and friend Nick ('Fuzz'), with whom Chris was climbing.

1. Preparing for a climb in the French Alps c. 1990. Camping at Les Chosalets campsite in Argentière. Note the ex-army rucksack, and Dad's favourite climbing breeches. Dad commented to Fuzz and me how clothing had progressed as we were climbing in tracksters. Note also the "A" frame tents in the background which

these days are a thing of the past.

2. Pausing in the Vallée Blanche. You can see a couple of other tents in the background. A magical place, cooling off in the midday sun. Roped up (hidden crevasses) and approaching the Cosmiques ridge that takes you to the summit of the Aiguille du Midi.

3. The Vallée Blanche again; a superb and enormous bowl high up surrounded by peaks of the Chamonix Aiguilles. The hole in the snow was our access to unfrozen drinking water (of sorts). Dad filling up the water bottles for the following day before it freezes overnight.

4. Morning preparations before a crack at the Cosmiques Ridge after a bivouac at the foot of the climb. Note the strap-on crampons (very old technology!) and the Whillans sit harness, guaranteed to ensure no further children should you be unlucky enough to take a fall in it. I am sure he still has it lurking somewhere. Also the classic Joe Brown climbing helmet. This stuff would not look out of place in a Mountaineering Museum. Dad proving, however, that it's not what you wear, it's what you tackle and achieve that counts.

5. On the Cosmiques Ridge itself, a great climb on mixed ground; wonderful Cham granite (or "grennit" as Dad would say) and interspersed with snow and ice pitches. The climb culminates at the viewing platform of the cable car station. One feels quite smug while tourists take your photo as you clamber, as dignified as possible, over the safety rail. Dad had a small bloodied cut on his finger, which is not uncommon on granite, and a kindly Japanese tourist whipped out a plaster and administered first aid even before he could put down his ice axe!

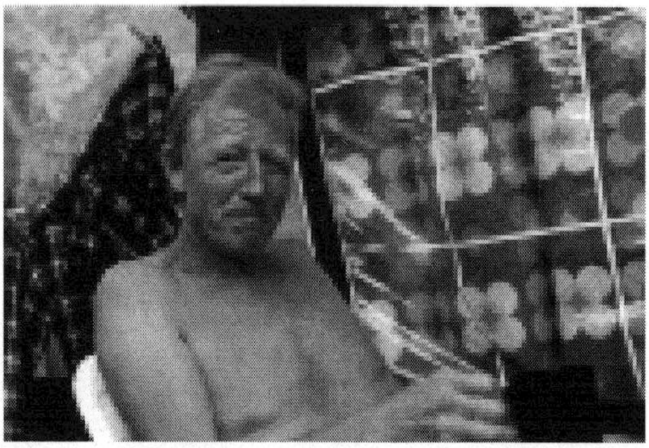

6. R&R day at the campsite. Again, note ex-army '58 mug. What do you think of the VW Dormobile awning with the cute curtains? Very Sixties! Happy memories.

On our family holidays, we travelled everywhere in our old caravan, towed by ever older campervans as the years went by. These expeditions usually included wild beaches, rivers and castles in France, and often mountains in Bavaria, Switzerland and Austria, all the best and highest of which had to be 'conquered.' One never quite grows out of that.

Day 25: Wednesday 19 May 2010

A Woman's Healing

07.40 hrs to 16.00 hrs
Odometer – 1,410 miles. Aviemore – Pitlochry (56 miles)

I woke just before my alarm at 6am, as is my habit, and managed to snuff it before it woke the rest of the dormitory. I packed the panniers, loaded the bike and left Aviemore at 7:40am this morning without a breakfast. I was feeling a bit low and disorganized, events overtaking me. Specks of rain suggested a wet day ahead, wrongly as it turned out. The gloomy weather reflected my spirits; so I stopped at Newtonmore for refueling. A brisk south-westerly opposed me, but I was growing used to that. Then, before the A9 reached Dalwhinnie, I took a little-used side road to the north of it that I had taken the last time I cycled this way. On that occasion 14 years ago it was a warm summer's evening. The road is now hardly ever used, the new A9 taking all the traffic. Countless thousands of rabbits were sitting on the road, soaking up its heat before bedtime. As I cycled silently along, this great carpet of fur politely parted just ahead of my front wheel and closed in silently behind me. The sea of rodents had no fear of me – why should they have? It was a surreal experience of what can happen when man is not in evidence and nature takes over again. Would this be the sort of thing to expect if the human population were wiped out by some epidemic?

I was still thinking about this as I rode through the Pass of Drumochter into Glen Garry, past Blair Atholl and Killiecrankie, and finally into Pitlochry at 4pm. When I found the bike shop a notice on the door said that the man had "gone away for a while". This was very disappointing. The odometer was invaluable not only for log-keeping but also for checking the route. I hadn't the time to hang around on the off chance that he would return, so I went to look for a bed for the night. Pitlochry is a busy and pleasant town, used to tourists. For me, this was unfortunate because every house advertising a bed was only interested in offering double rooms at double prices. It was only 5pm so I decided to ride on a few miles and look for a wood or hedge for shelter. I examined the map to look for a likely area and was stuffing it back in my top box when I found myself outside a B&B with a vacancy sign. I rang the bell and was welcomed warmly by the owner, Nancy. She took me into the kitchen and poured me a whisky while I answered her questions about what I was doing. She gave me a dressing gown and told me to put all my washing into the machine, topped up my whisky and cooked me a large meal with a pot of tea. As I ate, we had a long and engaging talk. It seemed to me she missed company. It had been a day of highs and lows, starting overcast like my mood; but then it warmed up and I discarded my Gore-Tex for the first time in 25 days. I got out of the headwind as I turned southeast over Drumochter summit, 110 ft higher than Shap, finally leaving the Highlands behind me... and then this kind woman, running a B&B in Pitlochry. She restored my faith in myself.

As I turned out the light that night, I wondered whether I could reach Edinburgh the next day (72 miles). I would try to contact friends there to see if they could put me up for the night.

* * * * * * *

On a different note entirely, Paul had told that an e-mail had just come in from James Muriithi [muriitjimmo@yahoo.com] of the Mountain Club of Kenya, who guided me up Mt Kenya three years ago. It was in my computer when I returned. Here it is verbatim, as an endorsement of this fine 21-year-old man who looked after me on Africa's second highest peak for three days. Please tell all your friends about him – or at least those who are planning such a trip.

"Hi Major,how are you doing?i just wanted to here from you because i have not heard from you a couple of months&also to alert you i have lowered the price for camping safaris&mounting trekking to be 100 dollars per day per person,this is to try to put myself in top possition to catch more client in this coming high season that is starting on july,so please try to market my business there to your friends&your relatives mostly this time of world cup.Major i wish you the best in every thing,you&your beloved family.

James,
Your mt Guide,Kenya."

Actually, I must be honest. My Kikuyu friend Jimmo also nearly killed me. I discovered later that he had been running a book with his mates in the Nairobi Company of Mountain Guides. They had told him that, aged 72, I'd be the oldest man by 10 years to have reached Point Lenana. I had no chance. He then bet he could get me up and down the mountain in three days instead of the normal five by missing an over-night acclimatization rest in the Austrian hut. This was pushing my powers of coping with altitude too far and I suffered a pulmonary oedema that could have turned into pneumonia the first night coming down, when we slept in wet sleeping bags that became encrusted with ice by morning. This came out during our drive back to Nairobi. Very African. But I am sure he's wiser now... Well, what do you think?

Day 26: Thursday 20 May 2010

Health And Safety On The Bridge

08.40 hrs to 19.00 hrs
Odometer – 1,512 miles. Pitlochry – Edinburgh (102 miles)

"If you can meet with Triumph and Disaster / And treat those two impostors just the same..." *R. Kipling*

I got a taste of both today. I awoke to disaster. In my hurry to get into bed, I had forgotten to set the alarm. (Paul suggested this was the sub-conscious winning the struggle for more sleep.) My body clock jerked me awake at 7:40am, an hour and 40 minutes late. I leapt out of bed, wolfed a slight breakfast and jumped on the bike, sped on by Nancy. In reluctant haste we parted, but I had recovered 30 minutes of the lost 100.

Now, you may find my accounts of the next couple of days rather dry and narrow in perspective. Perhaps this is because I had had little time or opportunity to rise above the harsh minute-by-minute grind of covering scores of miles with a heavily laden bike, on frost-damaged roads, over an endless succession of hills, always against a headwind of varying strength. A kind of poverty, if you like: "Road surface. Hills. Headwind. Ablutions. Eat. Sleep. Road surface. Hills. Headwind..."

Well, the first four hours were a triumph. I went through Perth – far more beautiful than I had imagined – and after 48 miles had lunch at 1:30pm in Milnathort. There were no hills, a good surface and no real headwind. It was warm and sunny and I was in a single shirt. I had averaged 12 mph and the day's target of 96 miles was looking less impossible.

But the gilt was taken off the gingerbread just after lunch at Kelty whence the road crossed a corrugated landscape requiring lowest gear in places. I took three hours to cover the next 15 miles to Inverkeithing and the Forth Road Bridge at 4:30pm. Not so much a disaster as a set-back.

Triumphs then followed disasters in quick succession. I had hoped to stay with friends of a friend, the Whites in Edinburgh; but their number was ex-directory. I rang Paul who said he would contact an old climbing friend, Martin Askey, and ring me back. Martin was delighted. Triumph. But I did not hear my mobile over the roar of the now-dense traffic. Disaster.

Then followed a psychological and hilarious triumph: crossing the Forth Bridge. This thundering dual carriageway was awe-inspiring. I paused and looked down 150 feet where steps descended to a street below: I was looking down the chimneys of North Queensferry. On the outer edges of the bridge were paths for cyclists and pedestrians. But there was a problem. On my south-bound side was a barrier, and I could see that some 50 yards further on someone had parked a drinks and snacks dispenser, presumably for the engineers working on the bridge. Except they weren't there. I therefore gingerly joined the heavy traffic of the south-bound roadway, hugging the fence. There were cameras and signal boards above each lane and after a while the one above the inner lane I was in signalled the lane had closed. The motor traffic duly pulled into the fast stream – leaving me to ride in style in an empty lane. I assumed there would be a blockage ahead, but that I would be able to negotiate it when I got there. Eventually the south bank was reached and the carriageways fanned out into a wide area. After a couple of hundred yards, out of a little kiosk leapt a 'yellow-bottle' with a flagging-down lollipop. I pulled over.

"Could ye nay see you was rusking life an' lumb riding in the motor lane? Ye should ha' used the cycle wee!"

"I couldn't, it was blocked. Someone had parked a coffee machine in it," I explained.

"Then ye should ha' gone doon the steps, under the brudge, up the steps the other side onti the cycle wee. Then at this end, doon the steps, under the brudge again, up the steps ti find yersel' heer. Ye could ha' been hurulled against the fence!" He seemed awfully cross.

I looked at him in disbelief. "Have you felt the weight of this bike? You wanted me to carry it a total of 300 feet down and 300 feet up because some nitwit had parked his coffee machine in the roadway?"

"It's Health an' Safety, d' ye nay ken?"

"Have you ever heard of heart attacks?" I asked. "They have something to do with health too, I believe."

"Och, awa' wi' ye, mon! Awa' wi' ye!" he cried, and stomped off to his kiosk.

So, I gang awa'.

Dalkeith was still 21 miles away by my reckoning. It was diametrically across the city. I attempted to find my way to it.

Vain hope! This was to be my next string of mini-disasters, ending in triumph. The road surfaces were not just appalling; they were bloody dangerous. At one point an extra deep pothole shook the bike so violently that my front box flew into the road scattering its contents. I laid the bike down in the road, stopped the traffic and, with great dignity, retrieved them before moving on. And of course, I got seriously lost, following road signs round the north that eventually finished in a dead-end road-works. I made my way back towards the centre and after several miles pulled over to a bus stop to ask for the road to Dalkeith. Blank looks. I had an awful déjà vu moment that someone was about to tell me the way to Tesco's. Finally, I asked if anyone could tell me how to get to open country; was the road I was on, which was pointing east, a good start? I added that I needed to get out of the city to sleep in a wood. At that point, a husband and wife in the queue said I would do no such thing: I would sleep in their house. I was effusive. They marked their map of the city and said they would come on by bus and meet me there in half-an-hour.

Charlie and Catherine were perfect examples of the sort of sympathetic generosity I had met over the last 1,600 miles, much of it in Scotland. They gave me more food and beer than I could put away, a hot shower, stimulating conversation, a bed, and breakfast in the morning before Charlie drove me onto the A68 Jedburgh road. I suspected Charlie wanted to drive me all the way as he was worried about the hills, and I had to insist he set me down. The previous evening we had spoken of our admiration for the superb qualities of our troops serving not just us but millions of people for whom they had no *natural* loyalty based on blood, nation or creed. And they backed their opinions with hard cash for *Help for Heroes*.

It had been an eventful 102 miles.

Day 27: Friday 21 May 2010

Generosity Of A Farmer's Wife

08.00 hrs to 20.00 hrs
Odometer – 1,585 miles. Edinburgh – West Woodburn (Northumberland) (73 miles)

I was up early and left Dalkeith at 8am, having said goodbye to the kind couple who had put me up for the night. The day was warm and still and the road surface was not at all bad. But the terrain was another matter: a long succession of ups and downs of increasing height to the border at Carter Bar. These Lammermuir Hills reduced my speed until I rode into Lauderdale, but after Jedburgh I entered the Cheviots. The hills were not particularly high – I think my summit at the border was 1,368 feet – but my road crossed the folds of the terrain rather than running along it, either on ridge or in dale. I called them corrugations. On the up gradients I only managed 3 mph; on the down gradients 12 mph. But since the distances up and down were roughly equal with little or no level stretches, GCSE students will confirm that the overall average in the hilly sections (that is, most of the day) was as low as 5 mph. Sadly, I couldn't cycle with my head in the clouds, whistling merrily, enjoying the scenery because I was forced to watch the deteriorating road surface like a hawk, to avoid winter's potholes while also dodging the passing traffic with the help of my nifty wing mirror. Impatient as I was, it seemed to be a day of very slow progress, though I wished I had had time to admire the views. However, by slogging away for 12 hours – including a break for lunch – I covered 73 miles. Over that terrain, it was respectable enough.

I arrived at 8pm at a farmhouse B&B, run by a delightful Irish woman who produced for me a huge sandwich and an entire bottle of red wine which I finished before bed time. The house was in a village called West Woodburn. A river ran quietly by and animals grazed and rested beside it. The soothing peace filled me, and the day's hardships were forgiven. I'm sure the wine helped.

****

At this point in the blog, Paul included another verbatim e-mail text from James Muriithi, my Kikuyu mountain guide. As it had something nice to say about me, I'd be a fool to miss the opportunity of printing it. It may make you smile, but clearly Jimmo is a supremely good judge of character. Judge for yourself:

"Hi paul,this is James again.Paul am very right when i say your Dad is one of the very few men who know the important of keeping there body in good condition&the way i see&hear him yuo can learn more from him.Not many old men can frontier to do such activities.Let you children spend time with him when they are free,they can learn many thing about life from him,he is very inteligent man.Have a good time together with your family,greet them all&tell your dad congraturition.

James mt tour guide."

Thanks, Jimmo. One day I will write up the log of that little expedition. I have fond, sharp memories.

Day 28: Saturday 22 May 2010

From Northumbrian Fells To The Plane Of Thirsk

07.30 hrs to 19.15 hrs
Odometer – 1,665 miles. Woodburn (Northumberland) – Durham and Northallerton (80 miles)

I was up early; the day looked bright and promising. Not only did the owner of the B&B refuse to accept payment: she and her family (whom she had rung while I was having breakfast) gave me an extra £40 for *Help for Heroes* – and another guest added a fiver! People's generosity is overwhelming, and how sharply it contrasts with the greed of so many of the Great and the Good that has preoccupied the press lately.

After so encouraging a start, it pains me to say this – I must sound like a whinging 'stuck record' – but physically today was an unusually hard one. On the road map, the A68 looks like an ideal line through Northumberland. But in fact, it is merely a strip of tarmac laid like a Roman road from A to B, with no engineering or earth-moving whatever. And one can see why: so hilly is the terrain that the cost of engineering would have been prohibitive, at least in the days the road was built. Between setting off from Woodburn and reaching Castleside 35 miles later I counted 29 hills that could only be cycled up in bottom gear 1:1, and some of them were more than a mile. There was no headwind, though, and the sun was so hot that by mid-day I had stripped to a thin shirt. The farm breakfast was good, and was to be the only edible food that day.

When I reached Castleside I rang Paul to say I would not make Ampleforth on schedule, explaining the corrugation problem. (My original plan had been to avoid these northern hills altogether by taking a longer detour up Tweedsdale through Moffat, Carlisle, Penrith and then east on the A66 towards Thirsk, but I was persuaded to take the shorter route to save time. Allowing myself to be persuaded was my mistake.) Paul and his wife Lucy examined the terrain map and advised me to run off the hills east-southeast to Durham before turning south on the relatively flat road to Darlington. I took their advice and was able to cover the next 50 miles to Northallerton in 6 ½ hours – 7.7 mph.

I had a slight accident just after Darlington. I swerved to avoid a huge pothole, hit the kerb and tumbled into a post-and-rail fence. My bare forearm acted as a brake shoe sliding along the fence rail and grazing it deeply. I was glad not to have been wearing my beautiful Gore-Tex jacket which would have been ruined: the forearm would soon heal. It took a while to extract all the splinters because of welling blood and I was a bit concerned about tetanus. I thought of using a small bottle of whisky, given me by Charlie Inness, to clean it; but mercifully came to my senses and avoided such a sacrilege. I called Paul, explaining this latest delay. He too came down strongly against wasting the whisky on 'a scratch' (my scratch, not his) and reasoned that any animal soiling would be on the inner side of the rail which was holding back a hedge. I wondered where he had acquired this deep reverence for whisky, and realized with a twinge of remorse that it was from me. Unconvinced, I used some of the whisky – albeit sparingly – and slapped a dressing on it.

I fetched up in Northallerton at 7:15pm and decided to spend the night at a large, run down hotel. However, it was cheap and available, and I had covered 80 miles. I was met at reception by the owner and her very overweight daughter who showed me the room. I was going to order in a pizza when the girl kindly said she would order me a curry as they were very good. I regret to say that the delivered product was repulsive, appearing to be the scrapings off other customers' plates, accompanied in an aluminium foil cup by a sort of industrial sludge. Honestly, I am not a fussy man – that I was so hungry is my witness – but I was unable to eat anything but the rice.

Then to bed.

Day 29: Pentecost Sunday 23 May 2010

Pentecost At Ampleforth And Night Beneath The Stars

06.50 hrs to 20.00 hrs
Odometer – 1,725 miles. Northallerton – Ampleforth, York and Selby (60 miles)

Pentecost Sunday was a superb day. By evening I reached Selby and settled into a secret bivouac in a wood just off the bypass. No one had seen me go in, I was sure, but I kept knife and phone (switched on) inside my sleeping bag. At one point as I was settling in, an alarm in a compound just through the trees went off. I wondered whether the compound was intended to be secure and a thermal sensor had detected my presence through the foliage. Perhaps dog-handlers would come sniffing. I lay doggo and after 15 minutes or so the alarm stopped. But first, here is the account of the daylight hours.

My own alarm clock woke me at 5:15am but I only left the hotel in Northallerton at 7am, spitting tacks. I had wanted to leave 40 minutes earlier and had arranged for someone to unlock the large garage in which my bike had been kept overnight, at 6:15am. But no one was up. I explored the whole premises and eventually discovered a stairway filled with rubbish. It seemed unlikely anyone would be living up there but I ventured up it anyway. On the landing a door was ajar but jammed. In the gap was the nose of a whimpering Alsatian dog. I pushed open the door opposite. I had thought the stairway a tip, but this room was in a class of its own. There were clothes everywhere, dirty dishes on the floor... and in the corner on a sofa the bedclothes stirred. It was like a scene from the cult movie 'Withnail and I.' The head of the girl who had locked the garage appeared from under the covers.

"I need the key to the garage so I can get my bike out. I need to be going now."

Sleepily she replied she would be just a minute.

Ampleforth Abbey

Five minutes later my bike was released and I set off for Thirsk and Ampleforth.

It had been a shock to me: the squalor that a young girl could allow her life to become. But worse than that, the woman who ran the hotel – but didn't live in it – was her mother! She had allowed her daughter to descend to this level of degradation. I wondered Whether the poor girl's obesity resulted from a lack of self-esteem consequent upon this evident lack of parental love. I felt very sad.

Nevertheless, on a glorious morning, I covered the 23 miles and arrived at Ampleforth just in time to gather my wits, meet my son Paul with his wife and children and join them in the Abbey Church for the monastery and school Mass of Pentecost at 10am. I had cycled 103 miles since my last square meal but I couldn't have been happier. The singing by the 600-strong school and monks was even better than I remembered it in my day. The Mass was beautifully celebrated, the Abbot's sermon was good – and there was an oblique reference to my effort in the bidding prayers. It was very moving. After Mass, we flooded out to the atrium for coffee. I met the other grandchildren with some of their friends, and was introduced to several monks, staff and people involved in running the school.

A son of St. Benedict

Eventually Fr Chad, the school chaplain, led us to the chaplaincy where people were gathering to hear my news. I spoke for about 20 minutes to 50 or so students and a few parents, telling how the inspiration had come from watching the TV programme 'Wounded' and mentioning that I had done three other such journeys, including the one to the tomb of the martyrs at Arles-Sur-Tech to thank them for my cure. People seemed genuinely interested and asked thoughtful questions. At noon we said the Angelus and I was able to mingle and chat individually. One or two students quietly gave me money, which was very moving. We then moved to a barbecue lunch, overseen by Miss Fuller and cooked by the Upper Sixth in my granddaughter's house, St. Margaret's, which was not only most congenial but very welcome, my only meal since breakfast the day before. Having been told of my craving, Fr Hugh even organised some fruit!

After that it was time for me to go. We went up to St Benedict's statue in front of the abbey where a bus-load of juniors had arrived from St Martin's, the preparatory school, with their Headmaster Mr Higham. A group of Irish visitors, wandering round the grounds, also came over and heard about the adventure and what the hullabaloo was about.

Finally, photographers with big lenses and (the icing on the cake) three traditionally clad Bagpipers from St. Hugh's arrived to send me on my way. They played 'Scotland the Brave' as I stood to attention. I then kissed my family goodbye, and with cheers of 'Good luck!' was away. What a send-off! It was superb.

I rode into the village and turned left at The Swan towards York at 2:45pm with renewed heart, strength and spirit. There were some initial steep climbs and, before I left the valley, I stopped to take a farewell photo of the Abbey and campus, looking back through a hedge from high ground. Memories from 57 years ago came flooding back, of a friend and me in the school borrowing a farmer's carthorse (my Irish friend Tyson was a fast talker) on a Wednesday afternoon. We had plodded along the same road and then up into the North Yorkshire Moors where the Hambleton Hills look down from the top of Sutton Bank. The view over the Vale of Thirsk from that vantage point, once seen, can never be forgotten. Far below lies Goremire Lake, said to be bottomless (naturally.) On that occasion, our nefarious mission was to detonate electrically a bomb I had made. It had become too hot to handle – the authorities were onto its existence – and its discovery would have spelt disaster. The explosion was unimpressive, but was almost nuclear in our estimation. In our efforts to remount him, the docile beast had decided enough was enough and delivered a hefty kick to my thigh. This provided me with the excuse to ride the whole way back, my grumbling squire leading the horse. In those days, the freedom to roam far and wide on Wednesday afternoons was a privilege strongly encouraged. Alas, academic studies are now given a much higher priority.

I arrived in York at 5pm and pulled into a pub in Gillygate for water. I ordered ½ a pint of beer to pacify the publican and chatted for a while with people at the bar. On my way out, people eating at a table stopped me, asked for my story and made a donation. It turned out that one woman's son-in-law had just returned from Afghanistan. I encountered such connections in almost every town where I stopped.

Riding easily through the city, I reached Selby bypass at 7pm and managed to transfer into cover without being seen. Good night on this day of the Holy Spirit!

Paul's family at Ampleforth

The Ampleforth Pipers' farewell

Day 30: Monday 24 May 2010

A Disappointment

07.00 hrs to 18.40 hrs
Odometer – 1,802 miles. Selby – Lincoln and Sleaford (77 miles)

I had set up my bivy on the outskirts of Selby and was in it by 8pm. The night had been hard but bearable. I had applied insect repellent to my face to stop the midges pestering me, and wore a woollen cap to keep them out of my hair. They woke me at 2am, the six-hour protection promised on the tube having expired, and I applied more to face and ears by torch light. I then slept again until woken at 5:15am by the alarm. I got up, packed the bike, brushed my teeth and was cycling by 6:40am. My aim was to get as far as I could, Sleaford if possible. In the event, I achieved this in 11 hours having cycled 77 miles.

Cycling past the Drax power station to Goole and along winding lanes to Scunthorpe, I was just becoming quite pleased with my route-finding when I got lost in that fair town... but fortunately not for long. Soon I was finding my way out towards that extraordinary Roman Road that is the A15. Overall, the going was good, with some very broken patches of road on an otherwise good surface. The wind was a light south-westerly, so had little influence on progress. However, the country was like the agri-deserts of northern France, but with hedges and walls. Mile after mile the road ran, hardly ever touching human habitation. There were sporadic hamlets set back from the road, but the land was covered in huge fields of potatoes and seed crops, with little grazing and no horses.

When I got lost in Scunthorpe I bought a banana and pear for breakfast. Lincoln was a doddle to ride through, and I had a shandy and lots of water mid-day. My previous meal had been the barbecue at Ampleforth, but I had faint hopes of finding shelter in Sleaford: of the few houses on the road not one was a B&B. When I got to Sleaford, however, I pulled into a Travelodge, on the off chance. To my surprise, for the first time this journey a Travelodge had a room – but at a price: £57 ! Nevertheless, I needed a shower and a good bed, so I paid up.

Grumpy Old Man with a banana

I then went over to the adjoining Little Chef where I was served the worst meal of my entire journey. My request for a few chips was ignored – I was given a mound of them – and the meat pie was stone cold in the center and covered in a sort of farmyard slurry. I think the "chef" was an East European, and appeared to have no comprehension of English or microwave ovens, let alone cooking. (Perhaps he had been unable to get a plumber's job?) I complained to the woman in charge and she at once said she would cross it off the bill. But as I was collecting my things together to go, two women came over, gave me £10 and told me they had just paid for my supper as well. As they had done so before I made my complaint, the promise of the manageress to cut the cost of the pie off my meal had been all my eye and Betty Martín. This woman was a liar and a cheat, and interestingly the only truly dishonest person I had met the entire journey.

I returned to my room, made some phone calls and wrote up my log. The previous evening when I rang my daughter Catherine, I spoke to Molly my wife. She sounded breathless. Catherine had said she thought she might have caught a chest cold as a day or two earlier she had lost her duvet during the night. I rang again in the morning and said that if the medics were at all worried she must go to hospital. I also rang Paul that morning and asked him to ask the family to pray for their mother. Later in the day, he rang me to say a competent doctor had checked and passed Molly as fit, but thought her heart rate a bit fast. This was some relief to me. Later I spoke to Molly again. She said she was missing me, but was otherwise fine.

Day 31: Tuesday 25 May 2010

James And Sheila, And A Solicitous Dog

08.30 hrs to 12.15 hrs
Odometer – 1,838 miles. Sleaford – Nassington (Northamptonshire) (36 miles)

This was a great day, though a short cycling one of only 36 miles. Hungry though I was, I could not face breakfast in the Little Chef of the night before; so I bought a baguette roll of ham and cheese at the garage. Either I had become uncharacteristically fussy or my stomach was rebelling against so much of the badly prepared food that had started south of the border; but this too was inedible plastic. The bread was half-baked, the chopped ham and finely grated cheese tasteless, and after one mouthful I binned it. What a bore I had become, I thought; but the odd thing was that, though hungry, food really did seem inedible... except fruit: I continued to long for fresh fruit.

So by 8:30am I was off. The day was pleasantly cool. I rang a good friend of Andrew my son, James Baile, who had kindly offered me a bed for the night and some expert attention to the bike. He is a great cyclist and a super athlete. Only the previous day he had run a half-marathon to stretch his legs, and in conversation admitted he had once ridden and carried his bike to Everest base Camp. His wife Sheila and sons Ben and Robert also enjoy cycling and active holidays, on one of which they met up with my son Paul's family.

James Baile and Deefer Dog

James met me half-way and after making me eat two bananas (for my cramps) led me to the house, in the grounds of a Prebendal Manor and tithe-barn by the church in Nassington, a gem of a village. There had been stone-age settlements there before the present buildings, some of which were about 800 years old. There is a wonderful 16th century pigeonry with several hundred pigeonholes in its cool, dark interior. The murmur of the birds induced a feeling of peaceful meditation as if one were intruding on the praying of the office in an abbey. (How God must love listening to his praying creatures, I thought.) The manor had long been associated with the bishopric of Lincoln. James took me to his house opposite the manor house. It was cool, stone flagged and ancient, a spiral staircase leading to the floor above. As we approached the house, Deefer Dog, a Collie, came to check me out. James told her I was a guest of honour and she busily led me inside. From there on, she took me in charge everywhere. When I carried my kit to my room she was sitting on the stairs watching me, her hind quarters on one step and her front paws on the one below. She didn't move out of the way as I squirmed past her, but then followed me up the stairs. When I went to the lavatory she nosed open the door (there weren't always latches) and sat watching me. This was a bit unnerving but there was no deterring her: she had her instructions from the master. Sheila later told me there were a few sheep in an adjoining field that she assumed were her responsibility. When her other duties allowed, she would sometimes jump into the field and marshal them from one corner to another to keep her paw in. A most engaging animal.

James gave me a good lunch – and fruit. Afterwards, he took me to a cycle shop and I bought a cycle computer to replace the dud. This time I chose a radio one rather than a hard-wired version because twice now I had found the latter were unreliable. So, now I had a functioning odometer again. Then I had a thorough sort-out of my maps and schedule while James very kindly checked and adjusted the bike.

The pigeonry at Nassington Prebendal Manor

Before long, Sheila turned up with the boys and set-to preparing a meal for a Christian Fellowship meeting in the tithe-barn for about twenty people, to hear an interesting talk on the Chester Mystery Plays. I chatted to some people at table, and then returned to the house to finish preparations for the morrow. Only the next day did I find that they had had a collection after I left, and I was given £85 for

Help for Heroes. People's kindness and support for the cause never ceases to amaze me.

I slept well that night. As I turned out the light, Deefer nosed open the door and lay down beside my bed to see that I came to no harm during the night. What more could I ask?

Day 32: Wednesday 26 May 2010

Niall Fitzgerald – A Close Shave – And An Old Soldier

08.00 hrs to 18.30 hrs
Odometer – 1,908 miles. Nassington (Northamptonshire) – Ware (70 miles)

I woke at 5:30am, had a bath and quietly packed and loaded the bike before doing some map-planning. I was joined by Robert and Ben who were preparing for a 'field day' on the coast. Sheila hurried them along as James and I had breakfast. I said goodbye to the family and James's mother, and James led me through the lanes to set me on the road running south to join Ermine Street, the Roman road later called The Great North Road, or A1. The countryside was lovely, English and cool, the surface perfect. I thanked James for all his many kindnesses and sped off alone down Ermine Street.

Before leaving the house I had arranged to meet a friend of Paul's, Niall Fitzgerald, at an RV. I was now heading there. But on the way I misread a sign, correcting it a few miles later and adding 20 minutes to my journey. So I was late when I got to the RV. Niall was forgiving and friendly, and we set off south. We were now into the 'bumpy' parts of Cambridgeshire, as we talked of family and cycling. Niall had done a tremendous amount of publicity work to get my efforts taken seriously, and I was most grateful for this. I couldn't even advertise a garden fête, and without the know-how of people like Niall and Paul and my five daughters, this thing would hardly have left the ground.

At lunch we stopped at the Queen Adelaide (God bless her) in Croydon, Cambridgeshire – a first class meal. On the way, I had snarled my gears and Niall had unraveled them. The lady behind the bar, quite rightly, said we could have no food until our hands were clean. We were sent to the Gents and on our return were told to turn our hands over so she could inspect both sides before we were permitted to eat. We two naughty boys then enjoyed an excellent meal in the sun, until Niall had to leave for Royston – "something about an appointment for an interview with a hairdresser – I don't know, the modern world moves too fast for me." (Niall, I am truly sorry. That remark, as you probably guessed, was inserted into the blog by your 'friend' Paul. I only repeat it here to refute it and undo some of the damage it may have done your impeccable reputation.) I thanked him for cycling with me, for all his work behind the scenes, and for sorting out my cycle chain.

I continued alone towards Ware. On the way, the effectiveness of the H4H sash proved itself yet again. A man drove past, pulled over and got out. He made the action look ridiculous, as if he were emerging from a toy car, one arm hooked over the roof to give him leverage. He was built like the proverbial door of a municipal convenience. He crushed my hand and asked what I was doing, so I thought I'd better tell him: my tolerance to pain is not what it used to be.

"I'm going to tell all my work colleagues about you. And persuade them to fork out."

He violently shook my arm until I feared for its continuing attachment to the shoulder. I didn't think many would decline his invitation, even if they did play in the front row of his particular rugby team. He was mid-forties with short dark hair; tall, wide and... gigantic. He effected re-entry into the tiny long-suffering car and roared off in a spray of gravel.

A while later I cycled into Royston. Throughout the journey I had been haunted by the risk from traffic. A mirror attached to my right handlebar had proved invaluable. In Royston, my fears were realized. I was cycling through the outskirts of the town and was aware of a lorry following me. Still well ahead of the lorry, I came to a traffic-calming pinch in the road. The lorry, however, decided to try to squeeze past as I was riding through the pinch. He knocked my mirror forward on its hinge and continued to edge closer and closer, forcing me nearer the kerb. I knew if I hit the kerb with my front wheel I would be thrown not left onto the pavement but right – under the lorry's wheels. There was a canvas cover over the vertical ribs of the lorry's flatbed, and as this cover slid along the end of my right handlebar, the ribs started shaking the handlebars from side to side. I struggled desperately to remain upright and moving – to stop and dismount would almost certainly have caused me to topple under the lorry – and just as I was about to fall the lorry's tailgate finally passed and I was able to re-establish control of the bike.

The driver of a car that had been following the lorry put his hand on the horn and roared off in pursuit of the driver, presumably to read him his fortune. It was one of the worst bits of driving I encountered. Usually drivers were considerate and sensible. The incident had been a close shave and I had been lucky.

I stopped to reset my mirror, then cycled on to Ware where two old gents sent me to the Old Vic – "it usually has rooms" and it had, for £35 with breakfast. I arrived at 6:30pm after 10 ½ hours on the road. I went to the local Tandoori because in my experience real Indian restaurants have always provided good food and service. This one was true to form... "Le Spice Merchant" (I didn't ask). The Manager, Mr Imran Chandahadry, approached during poppadum & chutney while I was writing my log.

"Excuse me; I see you are cycling for *Help for Heroes*. Were you a soldier?"

"Yes."

"Me too," he said.
I stood up.

He was the third of four generations of soldiers. His grandfather was in the 17th Lancers, a fact of which he was very proud. Like his father, he too had joined and become a Sergeant Major in the British Army before transferring to the Bangladeshi Army and being commissioned. His son is also commissioned in the same, as is his daughter. We saluted each other. He cancelled the service charge, contributed £10 on the spot and asked for an explicit receipt as a souvenir and memento. I had to insist on paying for the meal – we were soldiers and equals. On my way out, I passed some people next to the door who had been talking about H4H and Headley Court (I gather it had been in the news); one leaned forward and donated another fiver.

It had been a good day – a very good day. The total donated today was £37.80 and the total so far on the journey £700. The H4H sash had proved invaluable.

Day 33: Thursday 27 May 2010

Across Tower Bridge

08.30 hrs to 19.45 hrs
Odometer – 1,950 miles. Ware – Headley Court and Woking (night at Reading) (42 miles)

The day started overcast with drizzling rain. I set off after breakfast 8:30am and it was quite cold, but by mid-morning it had dried out and by 1 o'clock the sun had broken through, shining patchily with a light wind.

My route took me down the Roman road to the capital, round the inner ring road to the City of London, crossing Tower Bridge at noon, and onto the straight A24 towards Epsom. Compared to Edinburgh, the road surfaces were a doddle and the road signing excellent. Unlike Edinburgh, the density of traffic and the huge number of traffic lights made it necessary constantly to stop and start, but I made good progress and rewarded myself by stopping at an Italian restaurant in Balham (or Clapham?) for lunch. I couldn't face any more junk food, and ordered a hotpot of mushrooms and garlic and herbs in a small copper saucepan, with 2 glasses of good red wine. I deserved it, and the bill was very reasonable. While waiting for it I phoned daughters Annabel (who was in Greece) and Fiona, who told me I had been discussed by Ken Bruce and Chris Evans on Radio 2. Heaven knows how they got hold of my challenge (perhaps Niall or Paul?) but I was most grateful for the money-generating publicity. I must remember to thank them when I get home, I thought.

I pressed on through London. Quite suddenly the towns, seamlessly linked, that make up this great city, began to separate and thin into suburbs – Merton, Cheam, Ewell and so on. I followed signs to Epsom, caught sight of one to Headley and took it. That was a mistake: I should have stuck to the route I had mapped out. The countryside was now becoming increasingly horsey, with stables and paddocks and glimpses of the racecourse through the trees, and some very expensive houses protecting their owners from intruders with huge remotely-controlled gates. And hardly a soul in sight! Headley turned out to be a few scattered houses, bad roads and tall trees. I had spent a long time unsuccessfully looking for a sign to Headley Court when I spotted a workman. He directed me to it, and suddenly there it was. I clocked in at the guardroom at about 3:15pm and explained my business. The guard commander was pleased to see me and asked if I would like to be shown round, but I explained I had a prearranged guided tour the next day and more miles to put in today; so he told me how to get back onto the main road and I cycled off.

I then cycled on as far as I could in the time left to me. When I reached the area of Woking at 7:45pm it was getting late so I called daughter Vicky and her fiancé Andy who collected me in the van and took me to the house of Andy's parents in Reading. We noted the pick-up point and said that that would be my start point for the next day's cycling. I was introduced to Andy's parents, Tom and Pauline, who were most kind and welcoming. After a meal and a bath, I slept like a log. It had been quite a long day.

Day 34: Friday 28 May 2010

Headley Court

16.05 hrs to 21.10 hrs
Odometer – 2,009 miles. Headley Court, then Hook – Amesbury (59 miles)

This was a day of exhilaration and hope, a suitable finale to all the highs and lows, the ups and downs (literally), the pain and pleasure, frustrations, desperations and joys of this pilgrimage – probably the hardest of the four I have done. As I have said before, a journey like this is a perfect cameo of life, the pilgrimage we all have to make. The more fully we enter into it the more completely human we become; because avoiding its pains and cherry-picking its pleasures is simply not an option. Only a wholehearted acceptance of the package deal will cut the mustard. How each of us comes to terms with this adventure we are born into will depend on our character, background and beliefs. For me, the perfect example of how to do it is found in the life of Jesus and his journeying through Palestine with his small gathering of close friends. One of the uncertainties I had to face nearly every day as the sun sank low was where I would spend the night. The anxiety grew as the dusk closed in; and occasionally the only answer had been to sleep rough under the stars – the best nights, perhaps. I would look for cover from the wind and from casual observation (the soldier's word for such cover is a hide) and find a level piece of ground with an indentation for my hip, without which sleep is difficult. Then kick away the stones, spread the Gore-Tex bivouac bag with the sleeping bag inside and crawl in out of the cold with torch, knife, water and phone. Each time those words of Jesus came to mind: 'Foxes have holes and the birds of the air have nests, but the Son of Man has nowhere to lay his head.' I would commit myself and those I loved to God and fall asleep.

One other parallel a pilgrimage has with life is the people one meets on the way. This is not surprising because it is only our contacts and dealings with others that make us human. Making due allowance for the everyday irritations we feel that can make our relationships gritty at times, I can honestly say I don't remember meeting a single soul who was not *deep down* just plain good. And I met dozens, perhaps a hundred or so. Every one of them was in some way worth dying for. (I have just written that and the truth of it has hit me between the eyes. It stands.) I am sure that humanity is profoundly good. My favourite saint, Julian of Norwich, knew this. That is not to deny the existence of terrible evil in the world, but merely to show it in its true colours as an unnatural aberration, like cancer. It may sound naïve, but this realization, reinforced every day, was hugely encouraging and one of my greatest rewards. But I digress.

I had already cycled through Headley Court the previous day so Andy, Vicky and I drove to the Cock Inn, our lunch RV in Headley. My sister Janet and daughters Fiona and Madeleine were already there, with Madeleine's three children, and later we were joined by my cousin Mary. It was a lovely reunion. We ordered lunch, but it took so long to arrive that I only had 20 minutes to eat it and get back to Headley Court where I was due to join a party for a conducted tour. I got there a bit late, but need not have worried: others were even later. Soon a lieutenant colonel arrived to take us round. There were about fifteen of us from various organizations: medics, designers of special equipment, other charities and six connected with *Help for Heroes* – including two young ladies from the organisation who made themselves known to me and said they had been following my progress. Apparently, at that time I was the most profitable single challenger; and frankly, this astonished me. There were also three young men supporting *Help for Heroes* by cycling coast-to-coast across the USA, 3,250 miles. Sensibly, they would have a support team. They asked me about long-distance cycling, especially the factors deciding rate of progress, and I was able to help them. I admired their enterprise, which was in the planning phase, and envied their excitement.

We spent 1½ hours being shown every aspect of the place. It is a magnificent Elizabethan-Jacobean house set in splendid grounds with many additional buildings for new facilities coming available. It was left first to the RAF and is now used by all three services as a centre of excellence for getting soldiers back on their feet. I had been there as a patient many years before and much of it I remembered, but there had also been huge advances with fitness machines and cutting-edge medical technology. The staff, covering many disciplines from neurosurgery to physiotherapy, are world class.

The aim at Headley Court is to get each soldier able to lead as fulfilling, normal and independent a life as possible by the time he or she leaves. Every patient is given a recovery programme unique to his or her needs. We saw one soldier who had suffered sever brain damage from a grazing bullet, but had some definite motor faculties for which new equipment was being produced from the drawing board for his needs. Prosthetic limbs are designed and programmed precisely for the individual – at £17,000 a limb. But this is a drop in the ocean compared to the cost of full lifetime care that would have to be provided if he could not eventually walk. The whole atmosphere was as I remembered it – upbeat and hopeful. The place is inspiring, as are the people it serves.

And that was how it had been the entire journey: people going out of their way to support and help. To repeat, at heart, people are just plain good. But I have jumped ahead a bit. After the tour of Headley Court it was getting late – later than predicted – and I realized it would be impossible for me to reach Amesbury that night if I started cycling from where I had stopped the previous evening. Paul had booked me into a B&B in Amesbury and if I failed to get there, I would not make Gillingham on Saturday noon where a reception had been laid on. I therefore decided I would have to restart my journey at Hook instead of Woking: it would still exceed the target of 2,000 miles. I therefore called up Vicky and Andy in the van and they dropped me at Hook from where I resumed my journey.

Having started at 4pm with 60 miles to go I had to get a move on. I cycled on steadily on unknown roads until I joined the familiar A303 just after its junction with the M3. It was now just a matter of pedalling hard before it got dark. Approaching Boscombe Down, the light was fast fading and I switched on my road lights for visibility. On reaching the Amesbury roundabout right at the end of the day, within 5 minutes I was pulled over by two cars, as had often happened.

Car 1: 'Are you Chris?'

'Er, yes.'

'Chris Evans and Ken Bruce on Radio 2 have told us to stop you and give you money. Here you are, mate. You're bloody marvellous.'

Car 2: 'I spotted you on the road. Were you in the Army?'

'You bet.'

'I was in air defence – 12 Regiment, in the Gulf war.'

'So was I! Attached to 10 Battery.'

And so the conversation went on... ending in another note being stuffed into my hand. The heart sings.

The going had been good, but even so, in the hours left to me, I only reached my B&B in Amesbury by 9pm. I had warned the owner by mobile telephone that I would be late and he said that it was not a problem. He made me most comfortable and I slept well that night, albeit a little hungry as I had had no supper. My mileage had reached 2,009 and tomorrow would be my last day. It was an exciting thought.

Day 35: Saturday 29 May 2010

A Champagne-&-Beer Welcome

08.55 hrs to 12.05 hrs
Odometer – 2,038 miles. Amesbury – Gillingham (Dorset)
(29 miles)

The B&B had been excellent. But more than that, the owner refused to accept a penny in payment, in recognition of my efforts for *Help for Heroes*. (I took this to be a gift to me, not to *Help for Heroes*. There were two ways I categorized donations: to me personally if the giver made that clear, and all the rest went entirely to *Help for Heroes*. Each night I totted up the day's gifts to the charity and noted them down, before adding the money to my own. At the end of the ride I added up all the day's takings and sent a cheque for that amount to *Help for Heroes.*)

I had 29 miles left to run before reaching Gillingham by noon, so I allowed myself 3 hours and set off at 8:55am. It was raining, and as the morning went on it dried up for a while before reverting to a steady rainfall as I reached Gillingham. There was a small group at Milton-on-Stour who hailed me joyfully as I rolled up. Among them were the two Gillingham PCSOs, Nicky and Pete. (Later, I was told that Pete – who had met me completely by chance in Cornwall – had confided to Nicky that he doubted I would ever complete the ride, so shattered did I look. So it was good to find him waiting for me at Milton.) I then rode on into Gillingham followed by my police escort, up to the town hall and British Legion. There, a great welcome awaited me. First, there were some of the family – Vicky, faithful as ever, sisters Janet and Liz and brother-in-law Chris. Then there was the Lady Mayor, and Leigh Mason the president of the British Legion branch who welcomed me. They gave me a framed certificate from the British Legion in recognition of my contribution to RBL's and my common cause – the welfare of our soldiers, sailors and airmen. I was also presented with a bottle of Moët et Chandon – which I did not spray over the assembled people as is the custom of racing drivers and other rough-mannered folk! I accepted both with delight and thanked everybody for turning out to greet me. Jake Francis-Jones, a retired naval officer, said they were only there for the beer (but what can one expect from a matelot?) There was also a section of smartly turned-out army cadets. One of them had already decided to join the Rifles. The scoutmaster was there and gave me a warm welcome. From my church there were Fathers Martin and David with Betty, and many others from the church as well as from the other churches in the town. And I was delighted to see some old friends such as the O'Briens and Adrienne Kimber... so many others it is impossible to name them all. So forgive me if you are not on the roll of honour: your presence was heart-warming, I promise you!

James Mackain-Bremner started a whip-round raising £230, bringing my total road takings to £950. This well illustrates the generosity of all the people I had met. Having drunk some very fine beer from the beer fest and talked to many people there, I said goodbye and cycled back to my house where I parked the long-suffering bike. James then collected Vicky and me and took us to lunch in his farmhouse, where Anna and the three girls joined us on returning from a walk. We had a delicious cold lunch, with much laughter and talk about what had been happening in the last five weeks. Vicky then drove me home where we began to sort ourselves out.

It had been a great home-coming. In the night, I was racked by cramps which had made an unwelcome reappearance. But I thought I could probably cope with that.

The journey had taken 34 full days, of which 31 full days were cycling. The distance cycled was 2,038 miles or 3,280 kilometres if you're a fan of Napoleon (and juggle the digits a little.) The average daily distance was 66 miles – not great, but about right in view of the weight of the fully-laden bike... (and the age of the rider?) The longest day was 102 miles. With a support vehicle to take the load and find resting places for the night, an average of 100 miles a day should be entirely possible.

Meanwhile, contributions continue to swell the total raised for *Help for Heroes*. For me, the heroes of this trip are the countless generous people I met on the way and those who have supported it online and by post. At a time when moral leadership in our country has been brought low by so many, they pick up the flag and follow the example of our serviceman and women who restore honour to the land.